THE CALL

DAILY PRAYERS & PROMISES FOR THOSE WHO ASK, SEEK & KNOCK

KELLI RAMSEY

PRAYER IS...

Prayer is God's gift.
Prayer is a necessity.
Prayer is for everyone.
Prayer is what centers me.
Prayer is free, and it's freeing.
Prayer is soft, yet so powerful.
Prayer is the breaker of chains.
Prayer is redirection for the lost.
Prayer is not to be taken for granted.
Prayer is a weapon against the enemy.
Prayer is what saves me from darkness.
Prayer is healing for hearts, homes, and nations.
Prayer is peace and clarity as I learn to wait well.
Prayer is sincere, complete without complication.
Prayer is service in motion, helping me love others.
Prayer is not only asking; it's being in God's presence.

I'm _____, and for me,

Prayer is _____.

ISBN 979-8-9943584-0-5 (paperback)

Published by Sparrow Song Publishing

Design and Production by Credible Ink

First Edition 2025

Printed in the United States of America

God, thank You for my praying mother, Patti.

She saw Your vision for this book in me long before I did. Her obedience to surrender her life to You shaped who I am today. You've used her love, steadfast worship, and resilience to carry our family a mighty long way. Amen.

God. Words. Connecting People.

I'm deeply passionate about these three things. Years ago, I prayed for God to purify these passions. I longed for Him to breathe fresh purpose into my career as a communicator and intertwine it with my love for empowering people.

God answered that prayer by turning my Instagram Stories into a virtual altar. What began in 2023 as me sharing short prayers from my quiet moments with God, grew into a resource for those God had called into my circle and beyond. The prayers were simple: just a few white sentences on a black background. But while the format was minimal, the impact was not. I didn't realize at the time how the Holy Spirit was moving through those words, touching parts of people's lives that I knew nothing about.

At the start of 2025, I felt God's call for greater. And here, my friend, is my answer: *The Call.*

The Call is a daily prayer book anchored in the truth that communication with God is both an invitation and a response. It reflects three sacred dimensions: God calling us into relationship with Him, the call He has on our lives, and our call to Him through prayer.

My hope is that these prayers will not replace your time with God, but rather serve as a Spirit-led prompt for a more intimate, living conversation with Him that moves your heart, shapes your purpose, and frees you from strongholds. The margins and white space you'll find on each page are yours. Use them to write down your prayer requests, make your vision plain, and to capture your reflections and the words God places on your heart after each prayer. Let these pages become as personal as your relationship with Him.

As I finalized *The Call,* I was studying the New Testament and felt an undeniable assignment to incorporate Jesus' words into the book's foundation. His words in Matthew 7:7 inspired the subtitle: *"Ask, and it will be given to you; seek, and you will find; knock, and the door will be opened to you."*

This passage captures the essence of persistence, faith, and expectation in prayer. May it serve as your invitation to ask boldly, seek intentionally, and knock faithfully, trusting that God both hears and responds.

Friend, I pray *The Call* becomes one of your tools to restore your relationship with God, renew your confidence and clarity in His calling on your life, and revive your spirit. I pray you bring others into your prayer life by sharing the words that speak to your soul or to a circumstance they're facing.

Let us pray.

JANUARY

PROMISE

"The LORD is near to all who call on Him, to all who call on Him in truth." Psalm 145:18

Here is the reality: God never leaves our side. What shifts is not His presence but our priority of being in it. We create distance through misplaced priorities, distractions, and pursuits that pull us away from His heart. This promise reminds us that nearness is activated through calling on Him in truth. Daily, hourly, moment by moment, we close the gap not because He has moved, but because we return. God is already near; prayer is what awakens us to His presence.

JANUARY 1

God, I surrender this new year to You. I invite Your Spirit to move throughout each minute, hour, day, week, and month. Have full reign over my life and create in me a new heart and spirit. Lord, I lay down my heart of stone, my stubbornness, my agenda, my unbelief, my complacency, and the strongholds that steal my freedom. I pick up openness to Your direction and a willingness to follow where You lead. Lord, I'm believing You to move in mind-blowing ways this year. I'm returning to calling on You regularly in prayer and to answering Your call to fulfill Your purpose over my life. Amen.

JANUARY 2

God, I am blessed by Your omnipresence. You fill every corner of the universe yet still make it a priority to remain intimately close to me. Wow! Please move through me, positioning me in places and situations where Your light and love are most needed. Amen.

JANUARY 3

God, creating intentional space for time with You reduces anxiety and gives me a greater sense of fulfillment. Please guide me away from the "unnecessary busy" and things on my long to-do list that don't align with Your will and call here on earth. Amen.

JANUARY 4

God, You are the Father of exceeding and abundant blessings. And while I know this to be true, I've allowed fear, doubt, past pain, societal smallness, and the enemy's schemes to limit my imagination. I recognize that this limited view often begins with how I see myself. So today, I invite You to help me redefine who I am through You. Please remind me that I am a child of the King, and that Your greatness is unsearchable. Lord, I am ready to see my life and my possibilities the way You do: big, bold, and shaped by Your Kingdom, not my fear. Amen.

JANUARY 5

God, thank You for Your creativity in making me unique. You took time to make me a one-of-a-kind original. When the enemy's lies of comparison, imposter syndrome, or envy try to overcome this truth, please send me reminders through Your Word and signs in my daily walk of how wonderfully made I am. Amen.

JANUARY 6

God, our land is hurting. Our land needs Your healing power. Your Word gives us clear instructions on partnering with You for a healthy world: to call on You, humble ourselves, seek Your face, and turn from our wicked ways. Lord, please open our eyes, ears, and hearts to this calling. Please help us see that we have the free will and ability to make the world a much brighter place that more closely reflects heaven. Amen.

JANUARY 7

God, thank You for all You've given me and the meaningful work before me. Help me steward it well by following Your will, not the expectations of others. Show me the difference between generosity and being bound by others' demands. Please give me the strength to stand firm in Your guidance. Amen.

JANUARY 8

God, I worship You for being the victorious Leader You are. As I begin this new year, I'm putting the enemy on notice and declaring first and foremost that I serve You, Jehovah Nissi. You are the God who has already won the battle against darkness.

I declare a year of making the devil real mad, reminding him that he's under Your authority. I commit to walking in obedience and confidence, trusting that no weapon formed against me will prosper and that every evil attempt against my life, family, mind, and calling remains subject to You.

Lord, I release any fear or apprehension about where, how, or when the enemy may arise by remembering this truth: You are my light and my salvation; whom shall I fear?

Thank You for Your sovereignty, Your victory, and for equipping me for this spiritual warfare through Your Word. I stand under Your banner, assured that You are in control. Amen.

JANUARY 9

God, thank You for waking me up. If You did nothing else today, allowing me to experience another morning would still be more than enough. I'll show my gratitude by living like I belong to You. You can trust me with this new-morning gift. Amen.

JANUARY 10

God, You alone hold absolute knowledge, so I trust in Your promise to provide all the guidance I need. Father, forgive me for the times I've tried to take control of what You've already handled and for seeking counsel from others before coming to You. Today, I set my heart to trust You completely. Help me obey and follow Your direction every single time.

Amen.

JANUARY 11

God, I understand now. As I delight in You, You shape my desires to reflect Yours. The closer I get to You, the more my heart aligns with Your will, and my prayers begin to echo Your purpose. Amen.

JANUARY 12

God, thank You for Your protection that surrounds me as I step out in faith and embrace the courage You've placed in my heart. Thank You for being all-knowing, all-seeing, and in control of all things. As I move forward in obedience to You, please keep me safe—mentally, physically, and spiritually. Amen.

JANUARY 13

God, thank You for the inspiring examples in Your Word. As I reflect on Paul's life, I am in awe of his calm assurance in the midst of trials. Lord, I desire that same assurance, trusting that You are always with me. Help me surrender fully to You, letting go of fear and anxiety so that faith and obedience can lead me wherever You call. Amen.

JANUARY 14

God, thank You for divine evictions. You remove me from situations and places that no longer serve You or the gifts You've so freely given to me. Amen.

JANUARY 15

God, You created me on purpose. You saved me from darkness for a purpose. Please use me to uplift Your Kingdom and those whom You are calling me to serve. Open my eyes to where fleshly desires and worldly metrics of success are drawing me away from Your will. I'm all in, God. Have Your way in my life. Amen.

JANUARY 16

God, You are my faithful Provider, and I thank You for Your daily provision and new mercies each morning. Please forgive me for the times I've doubted, hoarded blessings, or worried about the future. Please help me to trust You daily, walk in obedience, and surrender control, knowing You will always provide. Amen.

JANUARY 17

God, thank You for working all things for my good. This heavy load was never mine to bear, so I release it to You, trusting Your perfect love to conquer every fear. Please remove offense, doubt, and any trace of darkness from my actions, thoughts, and words. Fill me with Your love and lead me back to my assignment. Amen.

JANUARY 18

God, Your Word reminds me that You are faithful and will complete the good work You began in me. I repent for the times I've rushed or doubted Your plan. Today, I place my life, purpose, and plans back into Your hands, trusting in Your perfect alignment. Thank You for being my divine guide and for all You have in store. Amen.

JANUARY 19

God, You deserve all the glory and all the praise. Please forgive me for the times I've withheld my worship and allowed my schedule and earthly priorities to take the place of the honor that belongs to You. I commit my life to being a constant praise break for You— in my private time with You, through my actions toward Your children, and the testimony I share. Amen.

JANUARY 20

God, today I'm reminded that anything I withhold from You holds me back from fully embracing the calling You have for me. Help me to release every part of what I'm trying to control, trusting that Your hands are stronger than mine. Amen.

JANUARY 21

God, thank You for always meeting me where I am. I no longer want to be led by my fleeting emotions, but by Your eternal truth. I long to draw nearer to You and experience the fullness of true joy that's not rooted in my circumstances, but in Your presence. Amen.

JANUARY 22

God, I want to live a life authentic to Your call for righteousness. I know that no amount of empty Christian activity can substitute for true relationship and pursuit of You. Let my life be marked by the evidence of Your Spirit. May others see Your fruits of love, joy, peace, patience, kindness, goodness, faithfulness, gentleness, and self-control in me. Amen.

JANUARY 23

God, I want to be fully present in Your presence. All I desire is You; all I need is You. Help me remove anything that disrupts our closeness. Whether it's my own self, other people, or plans made outside of Your will, remove them. Amen.

JANUARY 24

Lord, thank You for breaking me gracefully, for humbling my heart and reminding me that Your strength is made perfect in my weakness. Though it was painful, You kept me close, using it to pull me toward my purpose. Thank You for renewing my faith and leading me closer to where I'm meant to be. Amen.

JANUARY 25

God, I know my body is a vessel. Please help me protect it and the environment where You want to produce a miracle. Amen.

JANUARY 26

God, thank You for community. Your Word reminds us that when two or more agree about anything they ask for, it will be done for them by the Father in Heaven. Thank You for every opportunity to lift prayers in community. Give me courage and discernment to welcome others into my life, so that together we may bring the petitions of our hearts before You. Amen.

JANUARY 27

God, please grant me the discernment to choose not just good things, but God things—people, opportunities, and actions shaped by Your hand to make me a true disciple. In a world where good is loud, let Your Kingdom and righteousness be louder. Grant me clarity and the obedience to follow what is truly of You. Amen.

JANUARY 28

God, You prepare a table before me, even in the presence of my enemies. Lord, when I wrestle with my own sense of justice and the desire to teach lessons that only You can teach, please examine my heart. Convict me where I need correction and guide me in the way that honors You. Help me to release my burdens into Your hands and leave them there. Teach me to walk in love, forgiveness, and humility, trusting that You are working all things together for Your glory. Amen.

JANUARY 29

God, I lift up those who feel far from You—those who are burdened, brokenhearted, and crushed in spirit, believing it's impossible to find their way back. Lord, in this very moment, open their hearts to the truth that You are nearer than their own hands and feet, and that their circumstances or strongholds will never consume them because of Your unfailing love and compassion. Amen.

JANUARY 30

God, I long to show others the same mercy and forgiveness You've shown me. May my heart reflect Your heart in every relationship. Amen.

JANUARY 31

God, Your Word calls me to put my whole heart into the work I do, as if I'm doing it for You. I repent for the times I've grown lazy or failed to give my best. Please give me the discipline to stay diligent and the wisdom only to pursue opportunities that allow me to honor You with excellence, without compromise.

Amen.

FEBRUARY

"You, Lord, are forgiving and good, abounding in love to all who call to You. Hear my prayer, LORD; listen to my cry for mercy. When I am in distress, I call to You, because You answer me."
Psalm 86:5–7

God does not wait for us to be happy or perfect before He listens. Isn't that comforting to know? His love meets us exactly where we are—in our distress, our brokenness, our desperation—and transforms even our hardest moments into places of surrender to Him. We do not have to clean ourselves up before we come. We simply call, and He answers.

FEBRUARY 1

God, as we celebrate this month, we thank You for the rich culture, deep history, resilience, and fortitude of Your children. Through every trial and triumph, You have remained faithful, blessing us with a legacy of strength, creativity, innovation, wisdom, and an undeniable spirit of victory. Let us stand firm in the truth of our history, rejoicing in the impact we continue to make. We celebrate Your faithfulness, knowing that what You've built cannot be erased. Amen.

FEBRUARY 2

God, thank You for calling me into a deeper relationship with You. I want my life to reflect the truth that communication with You is both an invitation and a response. I will show up with a heart that is open, honest, and willing, trusting that You meet me in every quiet moment and every surrendered word. I'm ready for the restored confidence and steadied spirit that are unlocked only through intimacy with You. Amen.

FEBRUARY 3

God, I surrender to You my thought life and communication habits that fall short of Your righteousness. Search my heart, renew my mind, and align my words with Your truth. As I strive to reflect Your light, may Your ways be evident in both my words and how I speak them. Please give me the power to replace ego with encouragement and criticism with constructive support. Amen.

FEBRUARY 4

God, thank You for being my ultimate provider, for knowing the difference between my wants and my needs. You faithfully supply all that sustains my health, peace, and purpose. I trust in Your wisdom and provision. Amen.

FEBRUARY 5

God, thank You for being my strength. I pray for the confidence and balance that Your servant David had—bold in battle, yet a peacemaker. He defeated Goliath through faith and soothed Saul's torment through worship. Help me to walk in that same wisdom, knowing when to stand firm and when to bring peace. Amen.

FEBRUARY 6

God, thank You for the Abigails in my life, who walk in wisdom, righteousness, and grace, holding me accountable with love. Help me to be that same voice of reason for others, to act with discernment, and to lead with humility. Open my heart to receive wise counsel, to set aside pride, and to follow the path You've prepared for me. Keep me from rash decisions and guide me to walk in Your will. Amen.

FEBRUARY 7

God, please bring my spiritual life into order. Align my steps so that my energy and efforts are not wasted. Teach me to sow in Your way and with Your heart, so that I may reap a harvest that glorifies You abundantly. Amen.

FEBRUARY 8

God, I trust You with the parts of me that no one else sees. Thank You for always hearing the prayers I'm too ashamed to say out loud and the quiet whispers of my heart that I try to ignore. Amen.

FEBRUARY 9

God, thank You for blocking people, places, and plans that were never part of Your calling for me. Thank You for intercepting the devil's scheme and saving me from fires built to destroy me. Please grant me the discernment and guidance to align myself with Your mission to save and serve here on earth. Amen.

FEBRUARY 10

God, thank You for the gift of time. As I work to steady my heart from the pressures of getting everything accomplished, I give my schedule over to You and invite You to prioritize what's most important in Your eyes. Amen.

FEBRUARY 11

God, thank You for the gift of wisdom. It's so often overlooked, yet one of the greatest blessings You give. Today, I ask for the vast and immeasurable wisdom You gave King Solomon. Grant me discernment to know the difference between knowledge and true, godly wisdom. Help me not only to understand Your truth but to live it out in alignment with Your will. Guide my steps so that every choice I make honors You. Amen.

FEBRUARY 12

God, thank You for moments of stillness, rest, and restoration. Teach me to balance renewal with purposeful work. May I never take this stability for granted but use it to build according to Your will. Help me stay attentive to Your voice, knowing when to pause, when to be restored, and when to move forward with intention. Amen.

FEBRUARY 13

God, thank You for being You. That's it. That's all. That's the prayer, because Your presence is enough. Forgive me when I come with requests instead of reverence. You are almighty, holy, and worthy of all praise. Amen.

FEBRUARY 14

God, on this day when love is celebrated in so many ways, remind us that You are the source and example of perfect love. Teach us to love selflessly, to extend grace freely, and to cherish the people You've placed in our lives. Let our love reflect Yours—patient, kind, and unwavering. Amen.

FEBRUARY 15

God, You are just and faithful in all Your ways. You remember the deeds of the righteous and the disobedient alike. When I long to see fairness or resolution, remind me that Your justice is perfect and Your timing sure. Please strengthen my faith when I cannot see the outcome and help me to rest in the truth that You defend and restore what is Yours. Amen.

FEBRUARY 16

God, I pray for elected leaders and those who represent our voice and shape the policies that impact our daily lives. Lord, build within them a spirit of humility, justice, and compassion, and an unshakable desire to seek Your divine direction. Expose and remove corruption so that ethical leaders may rise and bring peace, prosperity, and unity to our communities. Amen.

FEBRUARY 17

God, thank You for new days, clearer vision, and renewed energy. Thank You for the perseverance to run the race that You marked out for me. Amen.

FEBRUARY 18

God, thank You for how personal Your call is. You aren't a passive listener but an active one, already at work as my prayers reach Your ears. Thank You, God. Amen.

FEBRUARY 19

God, thank You for the heart to contend for the Faith in the marketplace and on behalf of the marginalized. Please give me the courage to speak truth to power, secure in the confidence that You reign over all. Amen.

FEBRUARY 20

God, I want my prayer life to become a living conversation with You. I want it to move my heart, shape my purpose, and draw me closer every day. I will keep making space for You, Lord, by persistently, honestly, and expectantly calling on You. Amen.

FEBRUARY 21

Jesus, You told Your disciples, "The Spirit gives life; the flesh counts for nothing." As I plant this truth deep in my heart, let it be revealed in my daily actions. Open my eyes to discern between fleshly desires and Spirit-led ones that lead to eternal life.

Amen.

FEBRUARY 22

God, if You did it before, I know You can do it again. As I remember what You've told me and all You've done, I claim every promise You've spoken over me. I'm excited to watch Your will unfold, as I take one submitted step at a time. Amen.

FEBRUARY 23

God, You wouldn't tell me to launch out into the deep unless You had something there for me. So, here I am — ready to act in faith to live in Your deep love, plans, and blessings. Amen.

FEBRUARY 24

God, thank You for inviting me to ask boldly, seek intentionally, and knock faithfully. I take hold of this promise, believing that You hear me and respond in ways that align with Your perfect will. I will keep showing up in prayer with persistence, faith, and expectation, trusting that You honor those who pursue You with a steady and surrendered heart.
Amen.

FEBRUARY 25

God, You are the joy giver, and You know my heart's
desires. As I wait with anticipation for what's next.
Please teach me how to "wait well" by staying close
to You and seeing with spiritual eyes in this season.
Amen.

FEBRUARY 26

God, thank You for moments of celebration and reflection. Please grant us the strength to endure, the wisdom to unite, and the clarity to see each other as brothers and sisters in Christ. Lord, fill our hearts with understanding and forgiveness, even for those who seek to diminish the work You have done through us. Amen.

FEBRUARY 27

God, thank You for never giving up on me. Thank You for chasing after me when I wander—like the one sheep apart from the ninety-nine. Because of Your relentless love, I am never lost. I am always held by You as my strong and faithful Father. Amen.

FEBRUARY 28

God, please give me the wisdom, strength, and grace to draw healthy boundaries around my relationships. Help me identify the people who are pulling me away from the abundance You have for me. Provide strategies for disentangling without conflict and help me set parameters that keep me away from temptation. Amen.

MARCH

"And we know that in all things God works for the good of those who love him, who have been called according to his purpose." Romans 8:28

"Your grace and mercy have brought me through, I'm living each moment because of You..." I vividly remember singing that song as a child, the words flowing easily without fully grasping their weight. But as I grew older and experienced God's grace for myself, even in my failures and misuse of free will, I understood: He didn't just save me; He called me to a holy life. Not because I earned it, but because of His own purpose and grace. He blessed me when I didn't deserve it, and in response, my heart overflows with gratitude and a desire to honor that calling. His amazing grace saved a wretch like me, and now my life is my worship.

MARCH 1

God, thank You for being the God of compounded blessings. You know my every need, even before I do. Lord, You not only fulfill the desires of my heart that align with Your will, but You also reveal the areas where I need to grow so I can fully receive Your blessings. You open my eyes to deficiencies. You do this not to shame me, but to strengthen me. Thank You for always providing, guiding, and making a way. Amen.

MARCH 2

God, I no longer want to move in my own wisdom but in alignment with Your will. Please reveal any plans, ideas, or thoughts that are not fully in step with You. I trust You, Lord, and I am ready to listen, adjust, and follow where You lead. Let my good intentions be transformed into "God intentions."

Amen.

MARCH 3

God, thank You for being the Lord of audacious assignments. Sometimes this God-sized dream and vision feel too large for me to execute. But You have confirmed time and time again that, yes, this is Your will. Lord, I am returning to Your call, trusting that this dream is from You, the timing is appointed, and You will provide the strength and guidance needed to walk it out. I move forward confidently, with a new, purpose-fueled spring in my step. Amen.

MARCH 4

God, please build in Your children biblical discernment and a holy intolerance for false doctrine and false prophets. Just as Jesus warned His followers while on earth, these are the liars who perform great signs and wonders only to deceive.

Lord, help us be intentional and wise. Send Your Spirit to lead us in recognizing bad fruit masked by charisma and culture-pleasing soundbites. Build in us the courage to demand truth when a distorted gospel is being spread. Swiftly reveal those who masquerade as servants of righteousness and free the followers who have been caught in deception.
Amen.

MARCH 5

God, You are an awesome, mountain-moving God. Thank You for being the God of miracles and provision. Yet beyond Your provision, what I long for most is Your sweet, undeniable presence. I long to rest in the security, joy, and warmth that only You can provide. Please draw me closer and let my heart be fully aligned with Yours. Amen.

MARCH 6

God, I want to see the world and all that's before me, as You see it. Please open my eyes to see Your eternal truth that You save, heal, deliver, and love me unconditionally. Amen.

MARCH 7

God, You call me to true obedience, not empty words. I want my "yes" to be full, not hollow. Help me to follow through, offering more than words, but a life that honors Your heart and pursues righteousness.

Amen.

MARCH 8

God, thank You for women. Thank You for my sisters in Christ and for those who are still finding their way to You. Father, as we lift them up today, I pray You would give each woman a fresh wave of inner strength and dignity. May her character be her covering. Remind her that as Your daughter, she is enough and has enough in You. God, please remove any anxiety she feels about her future. Give her a full-bellied laugh of confidence rooted in her trust in You, and grant her a fresh peace about what lies ahead. Finally, send a host of angels and godly men to protect her here on earth, modeling Your love.
Amen.

MARCH 9

God, please forgive me for the times I let the toxic pursuit of perfectionism block my humility and dependence on You. I confess that chasing unattainable standards and being overly critical only leaves me feeling inadequate. Today, I lay down perfectionism and choose instead to pursue what Jesus called us to: holiness and completeness in love and character that is rooted in You, Lord. Amen.

MARCH 10

God, I'm declaring this season one of gratitude. I'm ready to replace complaints with praise and doubtful moments with a "Won't God Do It" spirit. Amen.

MARCH 11

God, despite the enemy working overtime, You reign supreme. Lord, I cling to the truth that You have already defeated the enemy. This emboldens me to look past external circumstances and the enemy's lies, choosing instead to focus intentionally on You and Your promises, Your truth, and Your chain-breaking power. Please strengthen my heart to stand firm in faith, knowing that victory is already mine through Christ. Amen.

MARCH 12

God, Your Word says that You have not given us a spirit of fear, but of power, love, and a sound mind. Please help me take fearful thoughts captive and immediately bring them to You so that Your peace can reign in my life. Amen.

MARCH 13

God, thank You for being the ultimate protector. Thank You for setting boundaries out of love and outlining them so clearly through Your Word. Though these limits may not always please my flesh, I find peace, purpose, and power when I live within them. Lord, I repent for the times I've pushed or ignored Your boundaries. Please teach me to embrace the intentional, supportive, and liberating limits You've set. Amen.

MARCH 14

God, Your Word tells us that, "A heart at peace gives life to the body, but envy rots the bones." I want to partner with You to break the chains of envy in my life. God, please open my eyes to the blessings You've given me. This awakening will make room for Your peace and my contentment to flow freely. Amen.

MARCH 15

God, thank You for the gift of rest. Thank You for moments to pause and return to You. Thank You for the permission to be still, to reset, re-evaluate, and realign with Your will. Amen.

MARCH 16

God, I trust that You have allowed this trial for a purpose I may not yet understand. Though I don't see the final destination of Your call, I trust You to guide me. I trust You to show me what to say, what to do, and what to release along the way. As I follow Your instruction and rest in Your provision, drive out every trace of fear and doubt. The victory is already Yours, and I choose to stand in that truth. Amen.

MARCH 17

God, thank You for being so intentional. I know that everything You allow in my life is designed to build my character, increase my dependence on You, or bring me into Your freedom. God, I trust You with all of me. Amen.

MARCH 18

God, I yearn for the heart posture of a child. For Your Word shows us that a willingness to trust, a readiness to be taught, and a lack of pretension are the way to enter the kingdom of heaven. Lord, I am ready to receive wholeheartedly. Please free me from my limited thinking or the cynicism that has plagued my belief in You. Amen.

MARCH 19

God, I know I don't carry this load alone. I'm drawing hope from Your presence and confidence from knowing that You will get the Glory in the end. Amen.

MARCH 20

God, grant me the balance to take in and give out as You ask of me. As I take in Your glory and blessings, I pray I can be a light to Your people. Amen.

MARCH 21

God, You are the ultimate provider. Lord, I've seen
You meet my previous needs according to Your Will.
As I strive to live a more righteous life, may my wants
and desires better align with Your heart. Amen.

MARCH 22

God, Your Word makes it very clear that "he who finds a wife finds a good thing and obtains favor from the LORD." Today, I pray for the single men whom You have called to be husbands and leaders of future legacies and households. Lord, I pray that their eyes and hearts would be open to the assignments and preparation You are working in their lives. Show them how to lead with wisdom, love with humility, and reflect Your heart in every season. Amen.

MARCH 23

God, today I pray for single women whom You have called to be wives. Lord, may they not wear their desire to be wives as their identity, but continue believing that first and foremost, they are Your daughters. You have called them to model the wisdom, strength, character, loyalty, and purpose of the Proverbs 31 woman. As You mold them into wives, I pray You are also molding their husbands into the men You have called them to be, worthy of a wife who is submitted and surrendered to You.

Amen.

MARCH 24

God, thank You for answering the prayers I never pray and hearing the words I'm too afraid to speak. Amen.

MARCH 25

God, today is a gift I'll never receive again. So, I stand confidently in the promise that You hold my future. Your promise frees me to live in each moment and not be consumed by tomorrow's worry. God, please guide me to be present and live within the Blessings of today, saving tomorrow for You to take care of. Amen.

MARCH 26

God, thank You for Your persistence. Even amid the noise, You find a way to find me.

I'm committed to shifting my routines, habits, and behaviors to be more intentional in my meeting times with You. Amen.

MARCH 27

God, teach me how to share my concerns with others in ways that honor You. Help me to speak truth with love, grace, and respect for Your children. Let my words bring peace, not division, and reflect the wisdom that comes from Your Spirit. Amen.

MARCH 28

God, I pray for the strong people in my life who are waiting on their miracle. Please renew their spirit. May they continue to serve others with a fresh confidence, fully trusting that You are working behind the scenes in their own lives. Strengthen their belief that You are preparing blessings for them. May Your peace free them to rest in the assurance that You have not forgotten about them. Amen.

MARCH 29

God, I'm sorry for the idols I've placed above You. I want to be free from every form of spiritual slavery, even if it means walking through a wilderness season away from what's comfortable and familiar. Though I fear the unknown, I trust You to lead me to my promised land. Amen.

MARCH 30

God, thank You for Your peace that rests over my life, covering me like the morning dew. It revives and restores me each day. Today, God, I want to be more intentional about hearing Your voice. This focus will drown out the world's overwhelming noise and provide fresh clarity and purpose. Amen.

MARCH 31

God, thank You for the blessings, lessons, and direction of this first quarter. But if I'm being honest, I'm starting to grow weary. Lord, please reveal to me which parts of this weariness are self-assigned tasks outside of Your will and which are part of the calling You've entrusted to me. I trust that perseverance matters in doing Your good work, and that in due season I will reap as I remain faithful. Amen.

APRIL

"For we are God's handiwork, created in Christ Jesus to do good works, which God prepared in advance for us to do." Ephesians 2:10

Jesus' death and resurrection placed us at the heart of God's redemptive mission. This calling was outlined before we ever existed. We are not wandering aimlessly; we are God's handiwork, crafted with intention and called to walk in the works He prepared long ago. Our lives are not accidents. They are appointments. You were never an afterthought. Every skill, passion, and experience was woven into you on purpose and for the good works prepared for you well before your first breath. Walk boldly, trusting that your calling is not random, but divinely assigned.

APRIL 1

God, thank You for all You've done for me. Thank You for a new day and for new morning mercies. Thank You for providing for me even when I didn't know what I needed. Thank You for second chances, for forgiveness, and for Your grace that continually covers me. Thank You for the favor that is never fair. I don't deserve what You do, yet You do it anyway. And for that, I am forever grateful.

Thank You for making me whole in You and for designing me exactly as You intended. Thank You for reminding me that I am enough. Thank You for the gifts You placed inside of me and the opportunities You create for me to use them for Your glory.

And God, if You never did another thing for me, You have already done more than enough. Amen.

APRIL 2

God, You're too good not to live a life of praise to You. I worship You with gladness, not because of what You do, but simply because of who You are. Let my worship be so contagious that it joins the command, "Let everything that has breath praise the Lord." May I never lack in zeal but stay energized by a spiritual fervor to serve You, Lord. Amen.

APRIL 3

God, please forgive me for doubting Your protection and provision. As I go throughout my day, may I be quicker to remember Your goodness and slower to complain. Amen.

APRIL 4

God, thank You for being my good Shepherd. Because of You, I shall not want. In a world that idolizes possessions and status, help me hold tightly to Your promise of provision. Teach me to live in contentment and find wholeness in You alone. As I dwell in Your presence, may goodness and mercy continually follow me. Amen.

APRIL 5

God, thank You for Your resurrecting power. Your light is victorious over all darkness. Just as You raised Jesus from the dead, You can raise me from my brokenness. In You, I am made new and filled with a fresh, living hope. Your love and sacrifice through Christ remind me to keep looking up, setting my heart on things above. Amen.

APRIL 6

God, thank You for loving me and wanting what's best for me. Help me to walk in a greater faith and trust in You. With this full faith, my heart's desires will align with Your desires for me, and there's nothing I want more. Amen.

APRIL 7

God, over and over again, You've met me in my valleys and freed me from the chains of shame. Because of this, I know You'll do the same for my brothers and sisters with waning faith or bound by chains of oppression. Amen.

APRIL 8

God, today I pray for the encourager. I uplift those who focus on the needs of everyone around them. We are grateful for their love and selflessness. But God we know they, too, may be struggling and waiting on a Blessing. So, I pray they find comfort in knowing that You hear their heart's desires and are pleased by their obedience. May they experience a renewed confidence that You are working on things in their lives and preparing blessings that are exceedingly and abundantly more than they could ever imagine. Amen.

APRIL 9

God, thank You for the opportunity to rest, reset, and reconnect with the people You've called me to love. May this week be marked by peace, productivity, and progress toward my assignment to bring Your Kingdom here on earth. Amen.

APRIL 10

God, thank You for shifting my prayer and my perspective. I no longer ask You to change my environment, but to transform my heart. Teach me to posture my heart in faith and gratitude, because my heart reveals my true walk with You. Amen.

APRIL 11

God, I know the enemy works feverishly to cast doubt on Your character. But You have equipped us with all we need to fight against the enemy and his lies. When the enemy is at work, grant me the discernment and discipline to cling to Your Word, promises, gracious fellowship and provision. Amen.

APRIL 12

God, I can't thank You enough for all You've done in my life and in the lives of those I love. When I struggle with contentment and comparison begins to blur the blessings You've already provided, please forgive me. Help me pause, remember Your faithfulness, and choose gratitude over envy. Teach me to guard my thoughts, to celebrate others sincerely, and to keep my heart fixed on what You've called me to do.

Amen.

APRIL 13

God, You are working all things for my good. As I learn the importance of waiting well, I take seriously the direction Jesus gave to Thomas to "stop doubting and believe." You've done it before, and You can do it again. You've done it for others; You can do it for me. Amen.

APRIL 14

God, I pray for those who feel far from You. I uplift those who believe too much time has passed for them to be loved or accepted by You. I bind that lie in the name of Jesus and cast it down to where it came from. Lord, set them free with the truth that no sin, no mistake, and no past decision is greater than Your love. May that freedom draw them back into Your arms. Amen.

APRIL 15

God, thank You for the gift of children and youth. Their light, faith, and innocence give us hope for tomorrow. Please forgive us for the times we have abandoned or overlooked these precious ones. Equip us with compassion, wisdom, and courage to defend and nurture them. Strengthen us to rescue those who are weak or in need and deliver them from the hands of the wicked. Amen.

APRIL 16

God, You remind me through the words of Jesus that "whoever walks in the dark does not see where they are going." Today, I recommit my walk to You. I want my life to be illuminated by Your guiding light. Amen.

APRIL 17

God, You redeemed me with purpose to serve, to lead, and to shine as Your light bearer. You didn't save me for my comfort, but for Your glory. Strengthen me to walk in my assignment. When You call, I will go. Amen.

APRIL 18

God, Thank You for reminding me that Your timing and Your blessings are always enough. Amen.

APRIL 19

God, I long to live the blessed life—one that follows Your commandments, passionately pursues justice, cares for those in need, and stands steady and fearless with a righteous heart. Lord, it can be hard, but it's worth it, and it's possible in You. Amen.

APRIL 20

God, Thank You for being the One who brings us back from captivity and breaks every stronghold that binds. Today, God, I lift up every person battling addiction or dependency, knowing that we all have things we turn to instead of You. I pray against those quiet addictions we can't yet name, the ones we don't even recognize as idols. Help us find in You what we've been searching for in substances, vices, possessions, titles, or people. I know firsthand that these things can never satisfy what only Jesus can fill. Lord, remove the desire from our hearts, the taste from our mouths, and the enablers from our paths. When we are tempted to find our value in earthly things, remind us that our worth, joy, peace, and comfort are rooted in You alone. Amen.

APRIL 21

God, thank You for Your absolute sovereignty. As You rule over all creation with wisdom and love, I'm assured that everything that touches my life has been allowed by You and will ultimately work for my good and Your glory. Father, please help me to endure with confidence, trusting and obeying You through every season. Amen.

APRIL 22

God, in the beginning, You created the heavens and the earth, and You called it very good. Thank You for the gift and beauty of nature for the places where we see You in the splendor of Your creation, in the lush green, and in the stillness of the land. Father, thank You for entrusting this earth to us. We repent for the times we have neglected to care for it, and today we recommit our attention, stewardship, and love to what You have placed in our hands. Amen.

APRIL 23

God, there will be days when life feels heavier than I can hold and nothing adds up. When those moments come, meet me in the middle of the confusion. Remind me that I don't have to understand everything to be held by You. Let Your presence steady my heart when answers don't come. Amen.

APRIL 24

God, thank You for Your never-ending love. There are seasons in my life when I feel like a prodigal child of Yours. But in my repentance and surrender, I return to You. You receive me with open arms and a compassion-filled heart, because in You I am made new. Amen.

APRIL 25

God, help me use my influence for good. Let my words and actions bring out the best in others, reflecting Your love and grace. May my faith inspire harmony wherever I go. Amen.

APRIL 26

God, thank You for the breath in my lungs, the power in my body, the gift of movement, the stamina in my steps, and the endurance in my spirit. Lord, I recommit my body as a living vessel to You and seek to honor You with all that I am. May my heart be a light, my mind remain steady, and my body stay strong. Amen.

APRIL 27

God, thank You for Your guidance. Thank You for being the Good Shepherd. Your Word tells us and experience shows that "whoever enters through You will be saved." Lord, please open my ears in this season that I may be able to differentiate Your voice from the voice of the enemy. This sanctified listening will position me to receive and walk in the Full Life Jesus secured for us. Amen.

APRIL 28

God, I'm done relying on my own understanding. I'm releasing my faulty perspective and urge to control everything. This submission will make room for You to work Your plans in Your time. Lord, I'm fully leaning on You and Your Sovereignty. Amen.

APRIL 29

God, thank You for Your coalescing power. As Jesus prayed in His final hours on earth that all believers would be unified, I echo that prayer today. In a world overflowing with division and offense, I ask for a great awakening to this calling and a renewed desire for us to "be brought to complete unity," so the world may truly see and experience Your love.

Amen.

APRIL 30

God, thank You for Your ability to replace chaos with calmness and exhaustion with an invigorating energy and opportunities to rest. God, when thoughts and to-do lists begin to overwhelm me, please grab my hand in that gentle, yet authoritative, way that only You can and bring me back to what You planned for me. Amen.

MAY

"Call upon Me in the day of trouble; I will deliver you, and you shall glorify Me." Psalm 50:15

Prayer is the bridge to deliverance. Every time we strengthen our prayer life and honor our time in God's secret place, we fortify that bridge between heaven and earth. God promises to rescue us from trouble when we call upon Him. Friend, to call is to pray. But His promise extends even further: after deliverance comes testimony. We are meant to walk across that bridge built by our prayers and share the story of what God has done. The world is waiting to hear how faithful He is.

MAY 1

God, Thank You for the gift of new seasons. Thank You for fresh opportunities to shed the old, to awaken what's been asleep in me, and to discover new life and new callings You've placed on my heart. As I enter this new month, please give me the courage and clarity to throw off anything You're asking me to release and replace it with every promise and opportunity You've prepared for me. Amen.

MAY 2

God, thank You for Your holistic care. From my spiritual health to my mental health, You desire to fill me with joy and peace. As I prioritize my mental health, I return to the power of prayer and ask You to ease my anxiety. Father, I rely on Your presence to renew my mind and restore my soul. I trust Your peace to guard my heart. Amen.

MAY 3

God, thank You for trusting me enough to call me to the work set before me. Today, I'm invigorated by the Scripture that calls us to do EVERYTHING to Your glory. Following this will shine a new perspective and greater purpose on the tasks that once felt mundane or ordinary. Working, engaging with others, and living for Your glory brings a new fervor and excitement to my life. Amen.

MAY 4

God, Your Word reminds me that my heart is the wellspring of life and that I must guard it. As I pursue sanctification—being set apart by You—fill me with wisdom that is both sound and sacred. Show me where I am serving others selflessly and where I may be stretching myself to please people. Lord, help me discern whether I am truly guarding my heart or simply putting up walls in disobedience to the people You've called me to love and serve. Amen.

MAY 5

Good morning, God. Thank You for a new day to experience Your wisdom and guidance. Please keep me steadfast in Your ways, so that I may live a life that honors and glorifies You. Amen.

MAY 6

God, Your heart and desire for biblical marriage is so clear throughout Your Word. Today, I uplift all marriages before You. May husbands honor their call to submit to You fully and to love their wives as Christ loved the church, and may wives honor their call to respect and submit to their husbands. Fill these marriages with Your love that is patient, kind, and enduring. Bind them with three-strand cords that are not quickly broken and serve each couple in whatever capacity they need, You, Father. For those desiring marriage, please mold them into the leaders and helpmates You are calling them to be. Amen.

MAY 7

God, You deserve all the praise! I can't thank You enough. I bow before You in reverence and awe with a heart on fire for You. I offer up my most authentic praise. You deserve nothing less. Amen.

MAY 8

God, today is going to be good! Thank You for the grace resting on my life. You call strength out of my weakness. So, I know whatever the world throws at me, I can face it with confidence because You are my guide. Amen.

MAY 9

God, thank You for mothers. Thank You for the women, both biological and spiritual, that You've gifted us. These earth angels have carried us through life while serving as Your hands and feet with love, humility, and compassion.

God, thank You for Your continued comfort and healing for those who have lost their earthly mothers by death or by absence in their lives, and for those who have lost children. Lord, please wrap Your loving arms around them as they encounter waves of grief during this time of year.

God, thank You for Your renewed hope for mothers facing infertility. Lord, we know that You open and close wombs, and we are trusting You to move through their hearts as they wait well on Your promise. Thank You in advance for their precious blessings. Amen.

MAY 10

God, Thank You for seasons of listening. I know the heart posture of a listener makes all the difference in living out Your Will. As I move my pride, plans, and worldly pressures out of the way, please quiet my heart so I can listen to You well. Amen.

MAY 11

Lord, You are the Living Water who satisfies my deepest thirst. Please fill me with Your Spirit; not just to meet my need, but until I overflow to bless those You have called me to. Amen.

MAY 12

God, thank You for the life You've given me. I know my purpose and the ways You'll use me may not look like everyone else's, but that's what makes my walk with You so beautifully unique. Lord, please remove any feelings of comparison or competition from my heart and fill me with confidence in Your timing, Your will, and Your divine plan for my life. Amen.

MAY 13

God, thank You for stabilizing and strengthening me. Because of Your sustaining power, I can boldly live out Philippians 4:13, confident that I can endure all things through Christ who strengthens me.

Lord, when I begin to doubt this Christ-empowered truth or grow discontent in the different seasons of my life, please infuse me with fresh strength and a heart of gratitude so I can remain steady in every season. Thank You that, in You, I am more than a conqueror. Amen.

MAY 14

God, I know that walking in faith doesn't mean life will always be easy. But it does mean I never have to face anything alone. When challenges come, please help me to see Your hand at work in the process and not grow weary or afraid. You are strengthening me for what's next, and I trust You completely. Amen.

MAY 15

God, thank You for the gift of friendship. Thank You for the people who uplift me, pray for me, and remind me of who I am in You. Please continue to bless my friendships—to deepen the ones that are rooted in You and to release the ones that no longer serve the purpose You've called me to. Amen.

MAY 16

God, thank You for the blessings that I can see and the ones that I can't. Thank You for the doors You've opened and the ones You've closed to protect me. Please help me to keep a grateful heart in all circumstances, knowing that You are always working behind the scenes for my good. Amen.

MAY 17

God, please forgive me for the times I've allowed busyness to drown out Your voice, and for the moments I've overextended myself by striving outside of Your plans. Help me to embrace the rhythm of rest You have designed so I can always find peace in Your presence. Amen.

MAY 18

God, thank You for another opportunity to grow in grace. Today, I choose peace over pressure, faith over fear, and purpose over perfection. Please help me to stay centered in Your Word and to see myself the way You see me: loved, chosen, and enough. Amen.

MAY 19

God, thank You for the joy that comes from knowing You. When life feels uncertain, remind me that Your presence brings peace that surpasses understanding. Help me to rest in that truth today. I want to find joy in the little things, to slow down, and to see evidence of Your goodness all around me. Amen.

MAY 20

God, You are the giver of perfect peace to those whose minds remain steadfast in You. Father, I'm ready to shift my attention from earthly remedies and temporary escapes that only pacify me to Your power that can make me whole. Teach me to renew my mind through Your Word, the Christ-centered community You've placed around me, the professionals You've ordained for my healing, and every tool You've equipped me with to cast my cares on You, because You care for me. Lord, I surrender my empty pursuits of wholeness apart from You and place every anxiety in Your hands. Thank You for the divine comfort and strength that restores me and brings me joy. Amen.

MAY 21

God, Your power calms raging waters. Please bring that same calming peace to my racing thoughts and comfort to the places in my heart that still ache. Remind me that You are with me in the middle of every storm. Amen.

MAY 22

God, Your Word reminds me that You preserve the faithful and set their feet in a spacious place. Lord, thank You for Your steady protection. You can trust me with an increase of responsibility in this season as You position me for greater. Amen.

MAY 23

God, thank You for the gift of the Holy Spirit living inside of me! Help me to believe in big things and dream extravagantly, living with a spirit of expectancy for You to do great things in our lives. Let our actions and words make Your name famous across the earth. Amen.

MAY 24

God, during this time, we honor the lives of the personnel who gave the ultimate sacrifice in service to our nation. We honor them with gratitude and reverence. Lord, we hold fast to the promise of Jesus: "Blessed are those who mourn, for they will be comforted." Please surround every family who has lost a loved one with Your peace, wrap them in Your comforting embrace, and remind them that You remain their protector and steady assurance. Amen.

MAY 25

God, just like the one who returned to thank Jesus, help me to come back to You with a grateful heart. When You move, heal, provide, or guide, let my first response be worship. Jesus said, "Your faith has made you well." Today, I choose that same faith that thanks You quickly and trusts You fully. Amen.

MAY 26

God, please help me hold on to hope. Even when I don't yet see the fruit of the seeds I'm sowing, remind me that You are faithfully multiplying every act of obedience for Your glory. Strengthen my trust that a harvest will come in Your timing and in Your way. Amen.

MAY 27

God, please teach me how to share my concerns with others in ways that honor You. Help me to speak truth with love, grace, and respect for Your children. Let my words bring peace, not division, and reflect the wisdom that comes from Your Spirit. Amen.

MAY 28

God, thank You for Your unwavering goodness. There is so much about my future that I don't know, but I know You are faithful. And that truth is enough for me. It's enough to tell fear and the enemy's lies that they're not welcome in my heart and mind. Amen.

MAY 29

God, thank You for being Jehovah Nissi. Though the enemy comes in like a flood, Your Spirit lifts up a standard against him. Remind me of this truth even before I step into spiritual warfare, because the victory is already Yours. Amen.

MAY 30

God, You are worthy of all the praise, worship, and honor. Lord, please forgive me for the times when I only come to You with a request or when I'm oppressed. I repent for making our time about what I need rather than who You are. Amen.

MAY 31

God, thank You for being the intentional Refiner and Purifier. When I face suffering, grant me a spirit that rejoices in the storm, trusting that You are producing perseverance, character, and hope in me. I surrender to Your transforming work. Amen.

JUNE

"Call to Me, and I will answer you, and show you great and mighty things, which you do not know." Jeremiah 33:3

No one enjoys a one-sided conversation, including God. This promise assures us that the Lord not only hears our call but responds with divine revelation, unveiling mysteries we could never discover on our own. Trust that God listens with sincerity and answers with intention. Accept his invitation to a deeper dialogue that transforms what we know and who we are.

JUNE 1

God, thank You for Your never-ending presence. The joy and strength I find in You is the ultimate goal for my day. It's the assurance my soul needs to stay content. When my mind begins to drift or crippling worry tries to set in, please gently point me back to You. Remind me of Your promise that in You, I find refuge. I look forward to resting in Your peace today.

Amen.

JUNE 2

God, I want to see my life from Your perspective. Please help me to shift my focus from what feels delayed to what You're developing within me. When I see through Your eyes, I'm reminded that there is purpose even in the pause, and growth even in the stillness. Amen.

JUNE 3

God, You make no mistakes. As I'm encouraged by this truth, I marvel at Your craftsmanship in creating each one of Your children. Your Word reminds us that before we were born, You were intentional about who we would be. Today, I pray that Your children are reminded of these truths and that nurturing their God-given, purposeful identity becomes a way to honor You and experience Your ultimate peace and clarity. Amen.

JUNE 4

God, I'm grateful that You don't wait for a new year to bless Your Children with new things—new relationships, callings, freedoms, responsibilities, and fresh starts. Lord, as I delight in the gift of the new things You're trusting me with, may I carry them with humility and gratitude, eager to share my testimony of Your grace with others. Amen.

JUNE 5

God, You call Your children to serve You by reaching others with Your truth. I'll be honest, evangelism takes courage, and boldness doesn't always come easily. But You are Jehovah Jireh, my Provider, who has supplied me with the tools to make disciples. I will strive to keep love at the forefront as the truest sign of who You are and who I represent. Please open my eyes to the purpose in every place and every relationship You've entrusted to me. Amen.

JUNE 6

God, You are holy, perfect, and pure. Lord, I realize that Your holiness is not passive but calls for my full surrender. So, I let go of control, lay down my pursuit of perfection, and confess that I cannot save myself. I surrender all. I trust Your authority as I yield to Your will. Amen.

JUNE 7

God, thank You for divine evictions. Thank You for removing me from situations and places that no longer serve You or the gifts You've so freely given to me. Amen.

JUNE 8

God, You are the author of new mornings, and each one is a reminder of Your sovereignty over all the earth. Please forgive me for the times I've taken the gift of a new day for granted—failing to recognize what a sacred privilege it is to wake up when others didn't. I will be more intentional about greeting each day with deeper gratitude and purpose. Amen.

JUNE 9

God, I praise You as Jehovah Shalom. The more time I spend in Your presence, the more peace permeates every part of my soul and my life. Father, thank You for renewing me internally. Even when circumstances feel heavy and external factors seem bleak, I am finding a new solace in You. Amen.

JUNE 10

Lord, Your Word is a safe place, and in it I'm reminded that "You hear the desires of the afflicted, You encourage them, and listen to their cry." So, God, today I pray especially for the distressed. I pray that they find peace and assurance in You as the ultimate helper, fixer, and defender. Amen.

JUNE 11

God, thank You for all the ways You train me to fully rely on You through testing and waiting. Please forgive me for failing some of Your tests. I repent and reposition myself to be used by You. Please bring me another test and help me respond properly. Amen.

JUNE 12

God, thank You for creating me in Your image. Once I unlocked this truth for myself, my identity and self-assurance through my confidence in You changed the way I operate daily. Lord, in the moments that I forget whose I am, please quickly remind me. Amen.

JUNE 13

God, thank You. God, I love You. That's it. That's all. That's the prayer, because You've done more than enough for me. God, You—outside of all You do— are more than enough for me. Amen.

JUNE 14

God, Your Word tells us that, "A heart at peace gives life to the body, but envy rots the bones." I want to better partner with You in breaking the chains of envy in my life. Please open my eyes to the blessings You have given me, so that Your peace may flow freely within me. Amen.

JUNE 15

God, please equip me for identity warfare. When the enemy works overtime to plant lies about my worth, my identity, or Your faithfulness, let those seeds find no soil in me. I pray for a Spirit of wisdom and revelation so strong that it becomes a shield around my mind and my heart. Amen.

JUNE 16

God, I call out every attack the enemy launches against the Call You have placed on my life. I know the enemy fears my purpose because he knows that when I walk in what You've called me to, his attempts for me to advance his agenda is destroyed.

Amen.

JUNE 17

God, thank You for restoring me and washing me white as snow. I stand confidently as a new creation in You. Even when the enemy tries to imprison me with my past or accuse me to draw me away from You, I will not agree with his lies. Your Word declares that the accuser has been thrown down, and because of that, his voice has no authority over me. His accusations cannot define me. I am forgiven and redeemed in You. Amen.

JUNE 18

God, I choose to believe in the future You have spoken over me. Let that belief quiet every fear, silence every lie, and calm every anxiety the enemy tries to stir. Anchor me in Your truth, steady me in Your calling, and strengthen me to move with confidence and courage. Amen.

JUNE 19

God, on this Juneteenth, we come before You with hearts full of gratitude. Thank You for the precious gift of freedom as we celebrate the emancipation of African Americans. Thank You for the beautiful legacy this day celebrates, honoring the resilience and enduring contributions of the Black community to our history.

Lord, we revel in the rich culture and traditions, which infuse our lives with vibrant energy and spirit. Today, we celebrate with worship, coming together in joy and unity. We ask that You help us cherish these moments and recognize their deep significance. Amen.

JUNE 20

God, thank You for the fathers and father figures You've blessed us with here on earth. Thank You for being the ultimate example of how a father should love, lead, provide, and guide.

Lord, I ask that You breathe a fresh wave of strength and courage into fathers, reminding them that You are with them wherever they go. God, please soften their hearts and open their minds to fully submit to You. Urge them to place You at the center of their lives and decision-making so they can lead their families well. Be with the fathers who are drifting or distant. Call them back to accountability for the children You've entrusted to them.

Lord, I also lift up those who carry father wounds. Thank You for Your continued comfort and healing for those who have lost their earthly fathers by death or by absence in their lives, and for those fathers who have lost children. You are the healer of broken hearts. Amen.

JUNE 21

Father, Your truth is the only way. Revealed in Your Word and in Your character, this truth stabilizes me in a drifting world and grounds me on a firm foundation. Lord, Your truth removes all ambiguity and frees me to live and love with clarity and conviction. Amen.

JUNE 22

God, today I put on the breastplate of righteousness. Lord, thank You for this weapon in my spiritual armor. Because of it, my heart is protected from the enemy's attacks. This breastplate guards me from the sharp shame he uses to sever me from intimacy with You, weaken my confidence in my calling, and deceive me into believing that I am not enough.

Amen.

JUNE 23

God, thank You for the shoes of peace. I lace up tightly this part of my spiritual armor and the readiness that comes from the gospel of peace. This gospel empowers me for spiritual warfare, because I know and have lived the good news of Jesus Christ. Amen.

JUNE 24

God, thank You for the shield of faith. Father, this weapon, fueled by Your power, is all I need to extinguish the enemy's arrows. Satan's spiritual attacks don't stand a chance when my faith is built on You, Lord. Amen.

JUNE 25

God, today I put on the helmet of salvation, covering my mind with the truth that I am saved, forgiven, and made new in Christ. This helmet protects my thoughts, beliefs, perspective, and imagination, ensuring they remain rooted in You. Amen.

JUNE 26

God, thank You for the sword of the Spirit, which is
Your Word. Your precepts are my offensive weapon
against the enemy, piercing every one of his lies with
liberating truth. Your promises anchor my heart and
strengthen my spiritual armor. Amen.

JUNE 27

God, thank You for the gift of prayer and its power to engage the full armor You offer Your children. Lord, thank You for sending Your Son, Jesus. Because of His sacrifice, I can pray in the Spirit on all occasions and bring everything before You. Amen.

JUNE 28

God, thank You that the armor You have given me is activated through living faith. Lord, let my belief in Your Word produce action in my life. This action puts on truth, righteousness, peace, faith, salvation, Your Word, and prayer. May my faith be alive, expressed in obedience, and strong in spiritual warfare. Amen.

JUNE 29

God, thank You for always making a way. Please give me the courage to keep believing, the patience to keep waiting, and the faith to keep trusting that Your plan is greater than my own. Amen.

JUNE 30

God, thank You for the midday moments and the rejuvenating reminders You send that confirm I am Yours and I'm more than enough. I love You. Amen.

JULY

"I have told you these things, so that in me you may have peace. In this world, you will have trouble. But take heart! I have overcome the world."
– John 16:33

Jesus shared this promise of peace with His followers during the Last Supper. Can you imagine how much chaos, sadness, and uncertainty filled the air that night before the crucifixion? But Jesus had already set His plans in motion to overcome this worldly chaos by overcoming the world itself. And in doing so, He gifted us a deeper inner peace rooted in God. Friend, I pray these daily prayers put you closer to knowing this peace for yourself.

JULY 1

God, You are the Lord of new things. As we enter a new month, we embrace it as a fresh start. Whatever You're doing in this second half of the year, please don't do it without me. Lord, my life and heart are fertile ground for You to work. I'm ready. Amen.

JULY 2

God, thank You for being You. As I watch, wait, hope, and pray, I find peace in Your Presence. The opportunity to sit and talk with You, and to meditate on Your Word, is more than enough of a blessing for me. You are everything I need. Amen.

JULY 3

God, in this season of faith testing and building, teach me to be more judicious with my "yeses." I only want to go where You are leading and entertain what is aligned with Your plan for me. Amen.

JULY 4

God, thank You for the freedom we have in You. Thank You for breaking the chains of sin and granting us the gift of salvation through Jesus Christ. As many celebrate Independence Day, I also rejoice in the liberty to live in Your love and grace, knowing that we are no longer bound by fear or condemnation. May we always cherish this freedom and walk in the fullness of Your Spirit, reflecting Your light to the world. Amen.

JULY 5

God, despite the enemy working overtime, You reign supreme. And Your Word reminds us to set our eyes on things above, not on earthly things. I recommit to looking beyond my circumstances and the enemy's lies. I will intentionally focus on You and my pursuit of a sanctified life. Amen.

JULY 6

God, thank You for the lessons of this season. I can feel them leading to progress and a deeper dependence on You. I trust You to strengthen me through the testing of my faith. Amen.

JULY 7

God, thank You for community. Thank You for the special people You have hand-picked to journey alongside me, to lovingly correct, gracefully guide, and selflessly celebrate the blessings You shower on me. Lord, open my eyes, heart, and schedule to ways I can pour into them. Amen.

JULY 8

God, thank You for being so intentional. I know that everything You allow in my life is designed to build my character, teach me a lesson, or bring me into Your freedom. God, I trust that You fully hear my unanswered prayers. You are working on something greater. You are orchestrating my life according to Your wiser plan and perfect timeline. Amen.

JULY 9

God, I want to show Your love to those I meet. Please equip me to be Your hands and feet here on earth. Convict me when I stray from Your loving and compassionate example and open my eyes to where You want to send me. Amen.

JULY 10

God, thank You for Your divine testing and refinement. Though the crushing feels unbearable at times and my flesh still longs for comfort outside of You, the truth is that You care far more about the purity and condition of my heart than my outward actions. So, God, I invite You in to examine every motive, intention, and desire within me. Send the Holy Spirit to convict me when I stray, because all I want to do is live Your way. Amen.

JULY 11

God, You saved me for a purpose. Please use my gifts and talents to serve Your Kingdom and those whom You are calling me to serve. Open my eyes to where fleshly desires and worldly metrics of success may be drawing me away from Your will. I'm all in, Lord. Have Your way in my life. Amen.

JULY 12

God, thank You for the unshakable truth found in Your Word. Lord, as situations, circumstances, and seasons change, Your truth remains constant. As I walk through life, teach me to shift from earthly thinking to heavenly living. I want to align my mind, my choices, and my beliefs with You. Amen.

JULY 13

God, I honor You as the ultimate protector and provider for all of Your children. Lord, please forgive me for the times I try to take Your place in people's lives, trying to fix all their problems and burdens. In doing so, I forget to trust You fully and lose sight of the fact that You alone are sovereign and capable of handling all things. Amen.

JULY 14

God, thank You for Your great love and Your unfailing compassion. Even when life feels heavy and trouble surrounds me, I'm not consumed because Your love sustains me and Your mercy renews me every morning. Amen.

JULY 15

God, You are sovereign, and Your Word never returns empty. It never falls short and always accomplishes what You intend. Even when human timing or understanding can't fully grasp it, there is certainty and power in what You speak. Thank You for Your consistency and daily assurances. Amen.

JULY 16

God, Your holiness is greater than my helplessness. When things feel impossible, please remind me that nothing is beyond You. Your Word tells me that You are greater than every situation, that You show up and meet every need. Thank You for Your holiness, Your steadfast love, and the faithful way You show up for me every day, in every way. Amen.

JULY 17

God, You keep on getting better, and Your Word gives me the confidence that You are always watching, directing, and caring for those who trust and believe in You. Amen.

JULY 18

God, thank You so much for the gift of laughter. Thank You for its power to restore and lighten the load. I want to partner with You to find intentional joy and moments of pure, unfiltered laughter. Because when I take life too seriously, I unintentionally take You out of the driver's seat by carrying what You never asked me to hold. So, Lord, help me choose joy and seek the kind of laughter that flows from trusting You. Amen.

JULY 19

God, I want to position my heart, my mind, and my faith to bloom right where You've planted me. Please help me find contentment and fulfillment in this season, trusting fully in Your placement and purpose. Please quiet the restless thoughts that urge me to do too much and instead teach me to sit, watch, and wait, trusting that You are at work.

Amen.

JULY 20

God, change my heart, my thoughts, my habits to be more like You. I've lived this truth: The closer I get to the image of Jesus, the more freely Your love flows through me, the easier life becomes, and the more beauty I see in each day. But it all begins with my willingness to surrender to Your transforming power. Amen.

JULY 21

God, thank You for transitions. Thank You for the
opportunity to move from better to best according
to Your will. Through these transitions, please grant
me the clarity to identify the plan You are speaking
into my life and not the one that my flesh is using to
distract me. Amen.

JULY 22

Lord, I don't want to be ruled by fleeting feelings.
Help me draw nearer to You and anchor my heart in
Your presence. Teach me to make room for lasting
joy that isn't shaped by my circumstances, but by
the unchanging truth of who You are. Please fill me
with the joy that comes from walking closely with
You. Amen.

JULY 23

God, because You said it, I believe it. Thank You for being faithful to Your Word. Everything You speak will not return empty but will accomplish what You intended. I'm here, ready to walk in alignment with Your Living Word. Amen.

JULY 24

God, thank You for the sons You've placed on this earth to reflect Your protection, guidance, and love. Lord, I pray against every attack of the enemy on men. Strengthen them with courage, conviction, and unwavering faith so they can stand firm in You.

Father, I ask that men—married, single, young, and seasoned—step fully into the assignments You've entrusted to them. Remind them of who they are in You, break every stronghold that hinders their purpose, and lead them into the fullness of their calling. God, I lift up the next generation of young men. Let them look to You as their example, their source, and their strength. May everything they do be covered in love. Amen.

JULY 25

God, Your Word reminds us that whatever we do, we are to work at it with all our hearts, as if working for You and not for man. As I continue in routines that may feel ordinary or even overwhelming, help me remember that I'm doing it in Your name and for Your glory. Remind me that the seemingly mundane becomes meaningful when it's done for You. Amen.

JULY 26

God, thank You for the gift of free will—the opportunity to choose. Lord, please forgive me when I misuse or abuse this gift by choosing actions or decisions that disobey Your call to righteousness or mishandle Your children and the resources You've entrusted to me. As Your Word says, though I may make plans in my heart, You alone establish my steps. So I surrender my choices to You. Teach me to choose in alignment with Your will and bring my desires under Your command. Amen.

JULY 27

God, thank You for restoring me and washing me white as snow. I stand confidently as a new creation in You. Even when the enemy tries to imprison me with my past or accuse me to draw me away from You, I will not agree with his lies. Your Word declares that the accuser has been thrown down, and because of that, his voice has no authority over me. His accusations cannot define me. I am forgiven and redeemed in You. Amen.

JULY 28

God, thank You for fresh starts. Lord, I want to partner with You to prioritize only what will push me closer to the Purpose You've ordained for me. Please help me to be a good steward of Your gift of time, discerning when to lean into opportunities or tasks and when to shift my focus. Amen.

JULY 29

God, You are the Ultimate Healer. As Jesus urged Jairus, "Do not fear, only believe," I strive to live out this command today. In this moment, I place my trust in You, knowing that Your plans are always good and for Your glory. Grant me the faith to hold steadfast, the courage to face each day without fear, the assurance that You'll never leave my side, and the wisdom to see Your hand in all things. May Your will be done. Amen.

JULY 30

The Serenity Prayer
(attributed to Reinhold Niebuhr)

God, grant me the serenity to accept the things I cannot change, the courage to change the things I can, and the wisdom to know the difference. Amen.

JULY 31

God, You are faithful to save. I once was lost, but now I am found in You, Father. Lord, Your love lifted me out of the mud and mire and set my feet on solid ground. You gave me a firm place to stand and reminded me that true contentment and joy come from You alone, not from the world. Amen.

AUGUST

"The plans of the LORD stand firm forever, the purposes of his heart through all generations."
Psalm 33:11

God's plans do not waver in the face of human circumstances. Considering the fragility and brokenness of our human nature, this promise is a blessing. It reminds us that God's purposes are firm, reliable, and endure across time. Though we may stray from the path He has outlined, His plans remain unchangeable. Let's thank God for his eternal plans.

AUGUST 1

God, thank You for Your Word, which gives me daily guidance and sustenance. I repent for the moments I've looked elsewhere for strength and answers. Today, I recommit to turning to Scripture first, before any worldly influence. Amen.

AUGUST 2

Lord, thank You for the God winks You send. These little glimmers of hope remind me of Your provision and sovereignty. I love You. Amen.

AUGUST 3

God, I praise You as El Roi, the God who sees me completely. Search the hidden places within me and uncover my blind spots so You may cleanse what does not reflect You. Amen.

AUGUST 4

God, I want to be a good steward of every blessing You give—my time, talents, and treasures. Lord, when I operate with an ungrateful heart, please convict me. Help me to partner with You and open my eyes to all of Your gifts and Your presence around me. Amen.

AUGUST 5

God, thank You for the reminder of Your power and the importance of truly knowing You. Help me trust and believe in You, unlocking my true potential. Please free me from the limitations of my comfort zone and societal labels. Though it's scary, I cling to Your Word and timing for confirmation and strength. Amen.

AUGUST 6

God, Thank You for the gift of the Good News, the message of hope and salvation through Your Son, Jesus Christ. Lord, as I walk the path of discipleship, I seek Your guidance and wisdom. Help me to be faithful and diligent in sharing the message of Your Kingdom, and to do so with a spirit of love and humility. I ask for discernment, Father, to recognize when hearts are open and ready to receive Your word, and when it is time to step back and trust that You will work in ways that I cannot see. Amen.

AUGUST 7

God, thank You for Your continued covering. As David proclaims in Psalms 63:7, "Because You are my help, I sing in the shadow of Your wings." God, amid confusion, change, and calamity, I am learning to trust in Your protection and provision. Your promises unlock a joy that no man or earthly force can take away. Amen.

AUGUST 8

God, Your Word reminds us in Galatians 6:9 not to grow weary in doing good, for in due season we will reap if we do not give up. While my body is tired, my spirit and soul remain on fire for the work You have called me to do. Please move through me today by Your Holy Spirit, guiding me to what truly matters— what You are calling me to do. Remove distractions so that I may follow only Your way, only Your call, only Your direction. Amen.

AUGUST 9

Father, thank You for Your patience with me, and for the daily doses of discernment, truth, and sanctuary that keep my soul full. Thank You for the freedom that only You can give. Amen.

AUGUST 10

God, thank You for trusting me with the work You've called me to do. Today, I'm inspired by the Scripture that urges us to do everything for Your glory. When I follow this, it transforms tasks that once felt mundane or ordinary, giving them new meaning and purpose. Living, working, and engaging with others for Your glory fills me with renewed passion and excitement. Amen.

AUGUST 11

God, I trust You with my brokenness and unrighteousness, because You love me through it. Thank You for never giving up on me. Amen.

AUGUST 12

God, I confess that I've treated the commands found in Your Word as optional suggestions rather than the divine directions they are. I commit to taking Your Word more seriously; not just reading it passively but absorbing it deeply and letting Your teachings shape my way of living. Amen.

AUGUST 13

God, when impatience or doubt begins to rise, please remind me that You are not withholding good from me out of spite. You are shaping me, strengthening me, and preparing me for what aligns with Your will, in Your perfect timing. Help me trust Your pace, Your wisdom, and Your love. Amen.

AUGUST 14

God, today I put on the strength, joy, and love that
You promised all of Your children. And I dare the
enemy to try to take it off. He's been defeated by You,
Lord, and I can't praise You enough for the victory.
Amen.

AUGUST 15

God, thank You for trusting me with Your children and for calling me to build Christ-centered community. Through fellowship, You strengthen us, teach us to love one another deeply, and grow our spiritual endurance. Show us how to honor and uplift the gifts within those we're connected to. Please guide our hearts as we partner together to bring You glory. Amen.

AUGUST 16

God, thank You for believing in me when I couldn't believe in myself. Thank You for always desiring an intimate relationship with me, even when I drift. Amen.

AUGUST 17

God, thank You for Your Son, Jesus, who bore my sins so I could be restored to You. Because of Him, I can come to You at any moment of any day, fully seen, fully loved, and fully welcomed. Amen.

AUGUST 18

God, please forgive me for the times I allowed comparison, complacency, or fear to dim the light You've placed within me. As Jesus told His disciples, we are the light of the world. You set us apart to live in a way that reflects Your goodness. Empower me to illuminate my testimony and refine my actions before others, granting me the words, timing, and courage to share. Amen.

AUGUST 19

God, increase my appetite for Your Word more than the world's trends. May Your daily bread fill me with audacity and fervor to spread the Good News. Amen.

AUGUST 20

God, I want my communication patterns to be marked by righteousness. Please give me the power to replace ego with empathy and elevation and to turn criticism into constructive support. Amen.

AUGUST 21

God, thank You for making known the path of life. In Your presence, there is fullness of joy. Lord, help me become a more intentional steward of the joy You've promised Your children by guarding my heart and capturing anxious and harmful thoughts before they dictate my actions. Amen.

AUGUST 22

God, thank You for Your retroactive grace that reaches into my past, covers every sin, heals every wound, and redeems every loss. What I once carried in shame, You've turned it into my testimony. Amen.

AUGUST 23

God, You call me to true obedience, not empty words. I want my "yes" to be full, not hollow. Help me follow through and live in a way that honors Your heart with intention. Amen.

AUGUST 24

"Save me, Lord!" were the words Peter cried out as he walked on water toward Jesus. God, I often find myself praying the same prayer when the places You've called me to feel uncertain and the waves around me feel heavy. Remind me that the real saving I need is not from the journey, but from my doubt in You. For I know, whatever You call me into, You are faithful to carry me through. Amen.

AUGUST 25

God, as I grow in spiritual maturity, I realize that repentance is more than asking for forgiveness; it is wholeheartedly redirecting my actions to reflect Your light. Amen.

AUGUST 26

God, thank You for being Jehovah Nissi. Before I even step into spiritual warfare, I bless You and praise You, knowing the victory is already Yours. Amen.

AUGUST 27

God, thank You for new days and fresh starts. Please help me to be a better steward of Your gift of time, discerning when to commit myself to opportunities and when to shift my attention. Amen.

AUGUST 28

God, please grant me the strength to move forward when I encounter resistance or rejection, without frustration or discouragement. Teach me to value the time You have given me, to invest it wisely in those who are seeking, and to leave the rest in Your capable hands. God, I long for my actions and words to always reflect Your love, even in the face of challenges. Amen.

AUGUST 29

God, thank You for reminding me that Your timing is always perfect, and Your blessings are always enough. Amen.

AUGUST 30

God, thank You for sending Your son, Jesus, who came to seek and save the lost. There are moments when I feel distant from You, unsure of my footing, overwhelmed by the noise and weight of this world. But even when my heart wanders, Your love never stops pursuing me. Please restore what feels broken and remind me that I am never too far for You. Amen.

AUGUST 31

God, thank You for Your perfect positioning. I no longer ask You to change my environment; instead, I thank You for prompting me to adopt an intentional perspective shift. Please transform my heart's posture, for it shapes my walk with You and my trust in Your plan. Thank You for calling me to this place and season. You can trust me here. Amen.

SEPTEMBER

"But you are a chosen people, a royal priesthood, a holy nation, God's special possession, that you may declare the praises of him who called you out of darkness into his wonderful light." 1 Peter 2:9

Peter wrote this to Christians scattered in a foreign land, facing hardship because of their faith. Though chosen as a holy nation, they still faced persecution for following Christ. Yet having been called out of darkness into a living relationship with God, the light of the Gospel overcame the suffering they endured. Friend, if you're facing your own persecution or hardship today, remember: You've been called into that same marvelous light, and it's bright enough to carry you through any darkness you face.

SEPTEMBER 1

God, a new month calls for renewed worship to You. Nothing in my life is too small to give You thanks for. I was made to worship You, and I will praise You not only in the sanctuary, but in the quiet moments and everyday tasks of my life. Amen.

SEPTEMBER 2

God, I am so grateful that You are the God of second chances. Thank You for Your endless mercy and grace that renews every morning. You look past my failures and offer me redemption. May I honor Your grace by striving to live a life that reflects Your love and mercy. Amen.

SEPTEMBER 3

God, I praise You for the angels among us. Thank You for the ones You've assigned to guard me in all my ways. For the people who lead by example, love like You, offer wise and righteous counsel, and remind me that I am covered by a heavenly army. Please continue to surround me with Your protection, presence, and peace. Amen.

SEPTEMBER 4

God, I am humbled by Your patience and Your unwavering commitment to my growth and restoration. Thank You for seeing me not as the sum of my mistakes but as a work in progress, worthy of Your endless love and forgiveness. Amen.

SEPTEMBER 5

Lord, thank You for breaking me gracefully, removing what I held onto in fear but didn't need. Though it was hard, You kept me close, using my pain to pull me toward my purpose in You. Thank You for renewing my faith and leading me closer to where I'm meant to be. Amen.

SEPTEMBER 6

God, thank You for the gift of work and the strength to labor. I recognize that all I do is by Your grace and should be done for Your glory. Please guide my hands and heart to work with purpose, not just for earthly gain, but for eternal rewards. Help me to see my daily tasks as opportunities to reflect Your love and to contribute to the world in a way that honors You. Amen.

SEPTEMBER 7

God, I'm tired of letting worry steal my joy. I'm done overthinking and stressing over things that are out of my control, imagining scenarios that may never happen. Today, I want to partner with You, trading my worry for Your supernatural joy. Amen.

SEPTEMBER 8

God, You have prepared me for such a time as this and for the task ahead. Today, I am reminded that where You lead me, You will also equip me. As I embrace the truth that I am fearfully and wonderfully made in Your image, I reject the enemy's lie that I am not enough and the weight of imposter syndrome. I release these doubts to unlock Your power within me, allowing me to shine as Your child and fulfill the work You have called me to. Amen.

SEPTEMBER 9

God, You are faithful to begin and faithful to complete. Your Word tells me that You cannot disown Yourself, which means Your faithfulness never falters, no matter what I do. Please forgive me, Lord, for the moments I doubt Your Faithfulness or when I mistakenly measure it by human standards, which can be so easily shaken. Amen.

SEPTEMBER 10

God, thank You for home. Thank You for the roots that ground me and the history that shaped me. Thank You for the chance to remember how faithfully You have carried me through every season. Amen.

SEPTEMBER 11

God, You are Jehovah Shalom, our peace. Our world, our nation, our state, our cities, our homes, and even our own hearts need Your peace that surpasses all understanding now more than ever. Replace fear with courage, bitterness with grace, and division with Your love. Comfort the brokenhearted and strengthen those in need of Your healing power.

Amen.

SEPTEMBER 12

God, thank You for revealing the path of life to me.
Your word assures me that in Your presence, there is
complete joy. Lord, I want to be fully present in Your
presence. All I desire is You; all I need is You. Help me
remove anything that disrupts our intimacy. Amen.

SEPTEMBER 13

God, today I uplift the encouragers—those who focus on the needs of everyone around them, often putting others before themselves. We are so grateful for their love, their selflessness, and the strength they pour into others, even when they may feel drained themselves. But, God, we know that even the encourager may be struggling. They, too, may be waiting on a blessing, longing for their own breakthrough. So, I pray that amid their giving, they find comfort in knowing that You hear their heart's desires. Remind them that their quiet sacrifices are not unnoticed, and You are pleased by their obedience and faith. Amen.

SEPTEMBER 14

God, thank You for Your peace that rests over my life, covering me like the morning dew. It revives and restores me each day. Lord, I want to partner with You today, hearing Your voice with my heart. Without Your voice, the noise of the world overwhelms, but with You, there is clarity and purpose. Amen.

SEPTEMBER 15

God, thank You for always meeting me where I am. I want to be led not by my fleeting emotions, but by Your eternal truth. Please help me draw nearer to You and experience the fullness of true joy that is rooted not in my circumstances, but in Your presence. Amen.

SEPTEMBER 16

God, I lift those who are facing storms today. Please bring them comfort and shelter, reminding them that this storm will pass and Your light will shine again. Let them find peace in Your grace, mercy, and unfailing power. Thank You for being their constant refuge. Amen.

SEPTEMBER 17

God, You are the source of my strength, healing, provision, and purpose. Your strength is perfected in my weakness. I surrender everything to You. I lay down my anxious thoughts, my health, my plans, my relationships, my fears, and the concerns I have for others. I trust You with their well-being and the burdens we all carry. Lord, have Your way. Amen.

SEPTEMBER 18

God, this burden is heavy. Yet Your power and promise of deliverance give me hope. Thank You for the blessing within the lesson, even when it stretches me. And though I suffer in private, I will still praise You publicly before the breakthrough comes. Amen.

SEPTEMBER 19

God, Your Word instructs us to speak to one another with psalms, hymns, and spiritual songs. I want to make music in my heart for You so that it flows through my words toward others. Even in disagreement, help me to speak with gentleness and assurance so that my tone and my speech are a worship to You. Amen.

SEPTEMBER 20

God, the tension between pleasing people and serving You weighs heavily on me. Please help me let go of my need for approval and prioritize Your will above all else. Even when others overlook my efforts, remind me that You see what's done in faith and You are the one who rewards it. Amen.

SEPTEMBER 21

God, I feel the urgency of this moment and the weight of eternity. I know Jesus is our only hope beyond this life, and I don't want to take that truth lightly. Please strengthen my conviction to live fully surrendered to You, and empower me to boldly lead others toward salvation. May my life point people to Jesus while there is still time. Amen.

SEPTEMBER 22

God, in Your omniscience, You know all things. Even when I naïvely believe I'm ready to see the full picture of Your plan or the road ahead, thank You for withholding certain things from my view. Your intentionality shields my growing faith and keeps me close to You instead of running when the journey becomes difficult. Amen.

SEPTEMBER 23

God, thank You for the wonder-working power of prayer and the opportunity to come to You at any moment, simply to talk and deepen our relationship. Lord, thank You for the example Jesus set through a life marked by intentional and constant prayer. In His highest moments and His most difficult ones, He always brought everything to You. I'm striving for the same. Amen.

SEPTEMBER 24

Good morning, God. Thank You for a new day. I'm reminded that this day is a gift I'll never receive again. So, I stand confidently in the promise that You hold my future. This promise frees me to live fully in each moment, not consumed by tomorrow's worry. God, please guide me to be present and live within the blessings of today, saving tomorrow for You to take care of. Amen.

SEPTEMBER 25

God, thank You for the opportunity to slow down and be with You. Thank You for freeing me from the bondage of perfection when I come before You. I don't need to have all my thoughts together, because You've captured my heart and understand the needs I've yet to put into words. Amen.

SEPTEMBER 26

God, as I open my heart to Your plans, may Your guidance quiet my anxieties and fill me with deeper fulfillment. Lead me through my day, steering me away from "unnecessary busy" and the tasks that don't align with Your purpose. Amen.

SEPTEMBER 27

God, I pray for my brothers and sisters facing storms today. May they be fully awakened to their spiritual authority as Your children and declare, "Peace, be still," in Jesus' name. Father, meet them where they are. Please be with them in the storm and bring them through it safely. Amen.

SEPTEMBER 28

God, thank You for the meaningful work You've set out before me. Please strengthen my heart and renew my spirit as I walk in Your purpose. Help me not grow weary in doing good. I trust that in Your perfect timing, I will see the harvest of my perseverance. Grant me the endurance to press on and the faith to never give up. Amen.

SEPTEMBER 29

God, I don't want to rush through the seasons of blessings You've given me or overlook what You're doing in my life right now. Teach me to be content and present, no matter the circumstances, trusting that Your plan is always good. Amen.

SEPTEMBER 30

God, thank You for restoration and revival that I may energetically rejoice in You. Amen.

OCTOBER

"Then you will call on me and come and pray to me, and I will listen to you. You will seek me and find me when you seek me with all your heart."
Jeremiah 29:12–13

The God we serve does not have selective hearing. He calls each of us by name and promises to listen attentively when we call on Him. Yet the beauty of this promise lies in our part: seeking Him with our whole heart. This is no casual pursuit. It requires laying down our own agendas, our sinful tendencies, and our carefully constructed plans. It's only when we seek not merely His blessings but His righteous ways that we will truly find Him. The promise is sure; the question is whether we will come with undivided hearts.

OCTOBER 1

Lord, thank You for sending Jesus to save my life and model true humility. I pray for a heart willing to serve others selflessly. Please reveal any hidden pride within me and show me how to love and serve better. Amen.

OCTOBER 2

God, what a privilege it is to be Your handiwork. Thank You for crafting a purpose that only my story, gifts, and influence can carry out. I will honor Your intention behind my calling by stewarding my gifts and time well and casting down every form of comparison or doubt that seeks to make me question what You've placed within me. Amen.

OCTOBER 3

God, thank You for the assignment You've designed for me. Reveal the distractions and idols that compete for my attention and affection. Give me the courage to release them and the clarity to stay fixed on Your purpose. Equip me to live out my full calling. Amen.

OCTOBER 4

God, I honor You as Jehovah Rohi. Thank You for how You shepherd, protect, and guide Your children. I pray that Your defending and rescuing power finds those who are oppressed, abused, and hidden in harm's way. Father, Your Word assures us that You remain close to the brokenhearted and that You bind up their wounds. So even now, I pray for divine liberation for the marginalized, the troubled, the exploited, and the mistreated. May they find refuge under Your wings as You shield them from danger and protect their minds from fear. Give them courage, strength, and a clear path to safety, surrounding them with earth angels who will advocate, protect, and support them. And God, for every oppressor, we call for Your justice where silence has lived too long. Raise up bold warriors who will stand firmly against every form of abuse. Amen.

OCTOBER 5

God, today is going to be good! Thank You for the grace resting on my life. You call strength out of my weakness. So, I know whatever the world throws at me, I can face it with confidence because You are my source. Amen.

OCTOBER 6

God, thank You for Your perfect love. Thank You for showing Your face to me in my moments of insecurity and adversity, and reminding me that I am more than enough. I'm a child of the King. Lord, please send small reminders throughout my day that You are with me. I will make myself available to receive them. Amen.

OCTOBER 7

Hi God, no asks today, just praise. Thank You for being You. Thank You for being the Way Maker. Thank You for showing up and showing out in my life, time and time again. Thank You for being my safe place to rest my heart when it's hurting and my best friend to talk to about everything. Thank You for Your on-time provision. Thank You for a new day and the opportunity to show how much I love and appreciate You by loving Your children here on earth. Amen.

OCTOBER 8

The Serenity Prayer

God, grant me the serenity to accept the things I cannot change, the courage to change the things I can, and the wisdom to know the difference. Amen.

OCTOBER 9

God, thank You for Your Word that unlocks the Truth for our lives. You call us to address difficult issues with honesty and love. Lord, please give me the discernment, courage, and open heart to overcome fear and speak Your truth to those in power today. Amen.

OCTOBER 10

God, I pray against the spirit of hypocrisy that can show up in my daily life. Lord, I recognize that this inconsistency can weaken my testimony and, for some, distort who I proclaim You to be. Help me to fully align myself with Your ways before I attempt to correct others. And Lord, if You desire for me to walk out my shortcomings alongside others, please reveal that to me. If so, give me the humility to admit my faults and to journey with them in grace. Amen.

OCTOBER 11

God, I pray for peace to descend across the world. Amid darkness, Lord, please shine Your divine light to end the chaos of war and hate. Lord, I pray Your love, compassion, and safety over all the innocent impacted by senseless violence. Please impart a deeper understanding in troubled regions and for a swift end to the unrest. We trust You as the God who brings lasting peace and true resolution. Amen.

OCTOBER 12

Lord, grant me more endurance and patience as I run this race, knowing that the key to peace and joy lies in trusting You completely. Amen.

OCTOBER 13

God, thank You for Your unfailing love and forgiveness that lift me when I fall and graciously guide me back to where I need to be. May Your covering be my confidence, empowering me to step out with full faith in You. Amen.

OCTOBER 14

God, I hear Your call to rest. You never asked me to carry it all or to carry it alone. My full surrender frees me to breathe, reset, and trust You. Amen.

OCTOBER 15

God, thank You for the friends and family You've entrusted to me. Thank You for the special care, time, and intention You put into creating such beautiful souls and astonishing humans. I pray that each of them grows to live with a solid, immovable faith in You. Amen.

OCTOBER 16

God, equip me to contend for the faith by first uncovering everything in me that's not like You. Amen.

OCTOBER 17

God, You set Your children apart to be the light of the world. Please guide me to show up as someone who belongs to You. Guard my mind and my tongue from pessimism and guide me to stay open to compassion even when it's not my first instinct. May each of Your precious children I encounter experience a glimpse of You through me. Amen.

OCTOBER 18

God, I'm tired of placing bandaids over wounds I haven't fully released to You. Lord, I'm ready to lean into Your promise of complete, lasting healing by placing my whole faith in You. You are the Great Physician. You heal not only the body but also restore the soul. Please honor this step of faith and cover me with Your wonder-working healing power. Amen.

OCTOBER 19

God, I surrender my schedule and plans to You. Please slow down the parts of my life that I'm rushing to and through. Please replace my anxiousness with assurance that Your timing is perfect, and Your plan is far better than the one I'm trying to force. Amen.

OCTOBER 20

God, thank You for blocking people, places, and plans that were never part of Your calling for me. Thank You for intercepting the devil's schemes and saving me from fires built to destroy me. Please give me the discernment and guidance to join You in advancing Your Kingdom and carrying out Your work here on earth. Amen.

OCTOBER 21

God, You are the well of living water that never runs dry. Your Word reminds me that we do not live on bread alone, but on every truth that comes from You. Let these reminders draw me into deeper dependence on You in every circumstance. Amen.

OCTOBER 22

God, nothing touches my life without You knowing. And while the hardships I face can be painful, I trust that You use them to strengthen my spiritual maturity, prepare me for what's next in Your plan, and draw me into deeper devotion to You. Amen.

OCTOBER 23

God, Your Word reminds me that You are faithful and will complete the good work You began in me. I repent for the times I've rushed or doubted Your plan. Today, I place my life, purpose, and plans back into Your hands, trusting in Your perfect alignment. Thank You for being my divine guide and for all You have in store. Amen.

OCTOBER 24

God, thank You for these moments of renewal and the opportunities for refreshing that bring hope and clarity for the assignments ahead. In Your name, I claim that today will be filled with productivity, purposeful work for Your glory, and actions that bring Your Kingdom here on earth. Amen.

OCTOBER 25

God, You deserve all the glory and all the praise. Please forgive me for the times I've allowed my schedule and earthly priorities to crowd out the honor that belongs to You. I commit my life to being a constant "praise break" unto You. Amen.

OCTOBER 26

God, today I'm reminded that anything I withhold from You hinders me from fully embracing the calling You have for me. Help me not just to wish for a complete release of what I'm trying to control, but to take intentional steps to surrender it all to You. I invite You, Lord, to move freely in my life, according to Your will. Amen.

OCTOBER 27

God, I praise You as El Shaddai. You reign as the All-Sufficient One. Thank You for Your persistence, Your promises, and Your presence. Even amid the noise, You find me and sustain me through everything. Your abiding nearness is my promise of hope and restoration. I live in the security of knowing You will never leave me. Amen.

OCTOBER 28

God, I desire a heart grounded in contentment. Like the Apostle Paul, I want a steadfast faith that trusts You completely, knowing that I can do all things through the strength You give me. Help me let go of restlessness and envy and, instead, find peace in my current circumstance. Amen.

OCTOBER 29

God, thank You. That's it; thank You. Thank You for Your love that endures forever, for waking me up, for this new day. Thank You for blocking what was never intended for my good, for pulling me out of the fire, and for second chances. Thank You for who You are, Lord. If You never did anything else, what You've done is more than enough, and I'm grateful. Thank You for Your guidance, love, and protection. May my life be an unending expression of gratitude to You. Amen.

OCTOBER 30

God, I pray for a stronger spirit of resistance—not toward You, Lord, but toward the schemes of the enemy. The enemy may be cunning, but You have already won the battle. Please clothe me in Your armor as I stand against the battles of this earth. Guard me from spiritual wickedness, and cover my mind, heart, and spirit. Amen.

OCTOBER 31

God, remind me of the power of the Holy Spirit dwelling in me. Your Word declares that when we submit to You and resist the enemy, he must flee. So I pray against every spirit not from You and declare that it cannot stand in the presence of Your Spirit within Your children. Protect us before any harm or destruction can take root. Amen.

NOVEMBER

"For there is no difference between Jew and Gentile—the same Lord is Lord of all and richly blesses all who call on Him, for, 'Everyone who calls on the name of the Lord will be saved.'"
Romans 10:12–13

God's call is no respecter of persons. His invitation is universal, extended to all who confess Him as Lord and Savior. This promise challenges us to reflect the heart of Christ. This is a love that knows no boundaries, no favoritism, no walls. In a world growing more divided by the day, our calling has not expired; it has intensified. To follow Jesus is to love without limit, to call on His name, and to extend that same grace to every soul we encounter.

NOVEMBER 1

God, thank You for saving me. You did not deliver me from darkness to stay silent. Please give me the boldness and opportunity to share Your supernatural blessings with others. Amen.

NOVEMBER 2

God, You are a miracle worker who moved powerfully through Jesus while He walked the earth. Today, I surrender every mental, physical, and emotional ailment to You. I lay at Your feet both my own and those carried by the people I love, and by all Your children in need of healing. Like the woman with the issue of blood, may we pair our faith with action and meet Your mighty healing power with hearts ready to receive. Amen.

NOVEMBER 3

God, please build in Your children biblical discernment and a holy intolerance for false doctrine and false prophets. Just as Jesus warned His followers while on earth, these are the liars who perform great signs and wonders only to deceive.

Lord, help us be intentional and wise. Send Your Spirit to lead us in recognizing bad fruit masked by charisma and culture-pleasing soundbites. Build in us the courage to demand truth when a distorted gospel is being spread. Swiftly reveal those who masquerade as servants of righteousness, and free the followers who have been caught in deception. Amen.

NOVEMBER 4

God, You did a great thing when You created me. Please send me reminders throughout the day of how wonderfully made I am, and how Your light overcomes any lie the enemy wants me to believe. Amen.

NOVEMBER 5

God, thank You not only for my physical ears, but for the ears of my soul. Please grant me abundant grace to listen first and to discern people's hearts, rather than leaning into my fleshly tendency to form premature opinions. Amen.

NOVEMBER 6

God, You are the Way, the Truth, and the Light. In Your presence, darkness and deceit cannot exist. Lord, as You reveal hard-to-handle truths of people and situations in my life, please order my actions to deal with them in Your righteous way. Amen.

NOVEMBER 7

God, please make my spiritual weapons effective.
I give You full reign over my life to pull down
strongholds and break ungodly influences. Lord,
guard my thoughts and imagination from the
calculated and persistent schemes of the enemy.
Amen.

NOVEMBER 8

God, I honor Your unbiased love and unwavering faithfulness. Thank You for never showing favoritism, but for receiving believers from every nation who reverence You and walk in Your ways. Your call to be in an intimate relationship with us was made loud and clear when You tore down the dividing wall through the power of the Holy Spirit. Help us to fully embrace this holy invitation, trusting that no matter where we come from on this earth, we all belong to You. Amen.

NOVEMBER 9

God, thank You for community. Thank You for the special people You hand-picked to journey alongside me, lovingly correcting, gracefully guiding, and selflessly celebrating the blessings You shower on me. Lord, open my eyes, heart, and schedule to ways I can pour into them. Amen.

NOVEMBER 10

God, please comfort those mourning during this holiday season with Your undeniable presence. Please replace their sadness with assurance that You will protect and provide for them. Please replace their despair with a soul-warming hope that Joy is on the way. Lord, uncover opportunities for us to be Your hands and feet here on earth, showing love and compassion to those in need. Amen.

NOVEMBER 11

God, I don't want to rush through the seasons of blessings You've given me or overlook what You're doing in my life right now. Keep my heart focused on You, Lord, and help me find joy in each moment, knowing that You are with me. Amen.

NOVEMBER 12

God, thank You for being the ultimate Teacher in forgiveness. Your Word declares that biblical forgiveness is the release of the right to retaliate and the trust that You will deliver justice. Lord, forgiveness is freedom. Please reveal anyone I need to forgive, and open my heart to model the gracious, intentional, and even costly forgiveness You have shown me. Lord, I surrender my ill feelings toward them and redirect my anger into prayer for my enemies, releasing them into Your hands. Amen.

NOVEMBER 13

God, You are worthy of all the glory and all the praise. Please forgive me for withholding my worship and allowing my schedule and earthly priorities to rob You of the honor You deserve. Amen.

NOVEMBER 14

God, please forgive me for the times I elevate my race, sex, or socioeconomic status above my identity in Christ. Lord, whenever I'm tempted to idolize any earthly category, quickly remind me that every believer stands equal at the foot of the cross. God, I'm ready to fully embrace my Kingdom identity and walk in the radical unity You call us to. Amen.

NOVEMBER 15

God, thank You for answering the prayers I can't find the courage to pray and hearing the words I'm too ashamed to speak. Amen.

NOVEMBER 16

God, thank You for the gift of democracy, where the free will You've given us can be exercised with discernment and guided by the power of Your Truth. Lord, we acknowledge that Your throne stands higher than any earthly seat of power and that Your righteous agenda surpasses every human plan. With this understanding, empower us to do our part in selecting capable leaders who reflect Your Kingdom here on earth. May we call up leaders who fear You, walk in integrity, and reject all forms of corruption. For Your Word reminds us that when the righteous thrive, the people rejoice. Amen.

NOVEMBER 17

God, thank You for working all things for my good. This heavy load was never mine to bear, so I release it to You, trusting Your perfect love to conquer every fear. I will keep my eyes fixed on You, knowing Your joy is my strength and song. Guide me where You want me to go. Remove offense, doubt, and any trace of darkness from my actions, thoughts, and words. Fill me with Your love and lead me back to my assignment. Amen.

NOVEMBER 18

God, thank You for the entrepreneurial spirit You've gifted many of Your children. It takes a special person to steward Your call to business ownership. Today, I honor their craft, discipline, heart, and courage. I pray a fresh fervor over the dreams You planted inside of them, Lord. I pray for a renewed faith in each of these visionaries that they build confidently, trusting that You will make their path straight, supply all their needs, and rest knowing that the plans of the diligent lead to profit. Lord, You honor obedience and diligent work, and in Your divine timing, You expand our territory according to Your will. Amen.

NOVEMBER 19

God, thank You for Your reconciling power. This power reaches beyond individual salvation and unites entire communities. Thank You for sending Your Son to be our peace, bringing unity where there was once separation. Lord, as our society grows more divided, please turn our hearts back to the barrier-breaking blood of Christ. Anchor us in the unity only You can give. Amen.

NOVEMBER 20

God, thank You for the inspiring examples in Your Word. As I reflect on Paul's life, I am in awe of his calm assurance in the midst of trials. Lord, I long for that same confidence. I want to trust that You and Your angels are always with me. Help me to commit myself fully to You, knowing that as I step into what feels impossible, You will quiet my fears and my anxiety through Christ-centered faith. Amen.

NOVEMBER 21

God, thank You for being all-knowing, all-seeing, and sovereign over all things. And even with this truth, Lord, I confess that obedience is often harder than I want to admit. As I move forward, one step at a time, please keep me anchored mentally, physically, and spiritually. This deeper, unbridled trust is new for me, but I believe Your glory will be revealed as I walk with You. Amen.

NOVEMBER 22

God, I'm declaring this season one of gratitude. I'm replacing complaints with praise and moments of doubt with a "Won't God Do It" spirit. Please move through me, positioning me in places and situations where Your light and love and my testimony are most needed. Amen.

NOVEMBER 23

God, thank You for divine evictions. Thank You for removing me from situations and places that no longer serve You or the gifts You've so freely given to me. Your Word reminds us that You preserve the faithful and set their feet in a spacious place. Lord, You can trust me with increase as You prepare and position me for greater. Amen.

NOVEMBER 24

God, You are working all things for my good. When I face negativity or rejection, help me shake it off as Jesus' disciples did. I will continue forward with a joy rooted in You and a confidence fueled by the mission You designed. I trust in Your plans and won't be held back by others' opinions. Amen.

NOVEMBER 25

God, I want to partner with You to prioritize only what will position me closer to the assignment You've ordained for me. Please help me to be a good steward of Your gift of time, discerning when to lean into opportunities or tasks and when to shift my focus. Amen.

NOVEMBER 26

God, You saved me on purpose, for a purpose. Please use my gifts and talents to serve Your Kingdom and those You are calling me to serve. Open my eyes to where fleshly desires and worldly metrics of success are drawing me away from Your will. I'm all in, God. Have Your way in my life. Amen.

NOVEMBER 27

God, You are my steadfast provider. Thank You for Your daily provision and new mercies each morning. I am grateful for Jesus, the Bread of Life, who fills my deepest needs. Forgive me for the times I've doubted, hoarded blessings, or worried about the future. Please help me to trust You daily, walk in obedience, and surrender control, knowing You will always provide. Amen.

NOVEMBER 28

God, thank You for being the ultimate Restorer. You refresh the weary and satisfy the faint. Thank You for the gentle nudges and firm reminders to accept Your invitation to pause and return to Your presence. Please help me embrace the rhythm of rest that comes from dwelling in Your safety. Amen.

NOVEMBER 29

God, thank You for Your guidance. Thank You for being the Good Shepherd. Your Word tells us, and experience shows that whoever enters through You will be saved. Lord, please open my ears in this season that I may be able to differentiate Your voice from that of the enemy. This sanctified listening will lead me to the full life Jesus secured for us. Amen.

NOVEMBER 30

God, thank You for being the Restorer of lost time and the Father of irrevocable callings. Lord, I lift up those who feel the clock has run out on their purpose and assignment here on earth. Please send them an undeniable conviction that, as long as there is breath in their bodies, You can still use them. Remind them that now is the perfect time to reclaim their identity as Your handiwork, created to do Your will in the unique way You designed. Amen.

DECEMBER

"And my God will meet all your needs according to the riches of his glory in Christ Jesus."
Philippians 4:19

Friend, I know you think you know what's best for you and when it's best for you. I've been there too. But this promise grounds us in God's sufficiency. Just as He did for the Israelites wandering in the wilderness, God provided fresh manna from Heaven each morning, just enough for that day. In the same way, God will give us what we need when we need it. He knows what's best for us and what's good for us, even when we can't see it yet.

DECEMBER 1

God, I'm in awe of Your omnipresence. I'm captivated by how You fill the entire universe yet never leave me alone. I want to honor Your perpetual presence by living with holy awareness, walking in integrity both privately and publicly, calling on You throughout my day, and choosing faith over fear. Amen.

DECEMBER 2

God, thank You for being the Creator of "new things" and for making ways in the wilderness and rivers in the desert. I'm blessed that You don't wait on New Year's to bless us with fresh starts, relationships, callings, liberations, and responsibilities. Lord, as I bask in the beauty of new things, may I do so with a heart of humility and gratitude, eager to share a renewed testimony of Your grace. Amen.

DECEMBER 3

God, thank You for the breath in my lungs and the functioning of my body and mind. Please forgive me for the times I have harmed my body or disregarded it as the temple of the Holy Spirit that it is. Lord, I was bought at a price, and I honor that sacrifice by recommitting my body back to You. I will fill and protect this living sacrifice with what pleases You and brings You glory. Amen.

DECEMBER 4

God, thank You for Your ability to replace chaos with calmness and exhaustion with an invigorating energy. When thoughts and to-do lists begin to overwhelm me, please grab my hand in that gentle yet authoritative way that only You can, and bring me back to what You planned for me in that moment.

Amen.

DECEMBER 5

God, I love You simply because of who You are. While Your blessings make life sweeter, they are nothing compared to the wholeness, well-being, harmony, completeness, and flourishing that come from being close to You. Amen.

DECEMBER 6

God, thank You for my uniqueness. Through You, I am a one-of-a-kind original. When the enemy's lies of comparison, imposter syndrome, or envy try to overcome this truth, please send me reminders through Your Word and signs in my daily walk of how wonderfully made I am. Amen.

DECEMBER 7

God, the Christmas season has a beautiful way of reminding us that Your purposes and plans always prevail. Lord, You know my heart and desires so well. Please build my confidence in this season of waiting and expectation by reminding me that You always come through. When doubt clouds my belief, please point me back to Jesus, the greatest evidence of Your perfect will. The Prince of Peace, the true reason for this season, saved us all by Your divine direction.

Amen.

DECEMBER 8

God, thank You for waking me up. If You don't do anything else, allowing me to experience another day is more than enough. May I show my appreciation for this new day by living as I belong to You. Amen.

DECEMBER 9

God, I honor You and Your miracle-working power. Thank You in advance for how You will show Yourself strong, mighty, and sovereign in the recurring prayer that lingers on my lips and sits deep in my heart. Amen.

DECEMBER 10

God, thank You for saving me from darkness. I am more than a conqueror because of Your redeeming power. May my testimony draw others closer to You as I faithfully stand against the enemy and walk in the victory You've already secured. Amen.

DECEMBER 11

God, I am so grateful for how You reveal Your blessings at just the right moment. Thank You for Your steady provision. You are wise beyond my comprehension, and You never place more on me than I can bear, even when my ego and ungrateful flesh try to deceive me. Help me to remain disciplined and live in the joy of each new day, trusting fully that You will provide exactly what I need. Amen.

DECEMBER 12

God, You are all I need. Please erase every substitute. Lord, I invite You to remove any people, places, desires, or possessions I try to put in Your place or use to fill the voids only You can satisfy. Amen.

DECEMBER 13

God, as we wait in anticipation for the newborn King, the light that shatters all darkness, I am reminded that You have called us to be the light of the world. Even when things feel tough, may we remember that we are still called to be Your hands and feet. Show us how to show up. Amen.

DECEMBER 14

God, I no longer want to be controlled by my temporary feelings and emotions. Instead, I desire to draw nearer to You and live in the fullness Your pure joy. Please guide me to make room for more moments rooted in Your presence. Amen.

DECEMBER 15

Lord, thank You for the God winks You send. These little glimmers of hope remind me of Your provision and sovereignty. I love You. Amen.

DECEMBER 16

God, I confess that I've treated the commands found in Your Word as optional suggestions rather than the divine directions they are. I commit to taking Your Word more seriously; not just reading it passively but absorbing it deeply and letting Your teachings shape my way of living. Amen.

DECEMBER 17

God, thank You for modeling the purest form of sacrificial, nonjudgmental love. Please let that same love reshape my heart, soften my responses, and overflow to everyone around me. Amen.

DECEMBER 18

God, thank You for so clearly showing me in Your Word what it means to walk in the Spirit. I want to be more intentional about walking in love, joy, peace, patience, kindness, goodness, faithfulness, gentleness, and self-control. I know that prioritizing these behaviors will produce godly character within me and shape a life truly worth living. Amen.

DECEMBER 19

God, Your timing is perfect, and I am so grateful for how You reveal Your blessings at just the right moment. Thank You for Your steady and subtle works of grace and provision. Help me to remain disciplined and live in the joy of each new day, trusting fully that You will provide exactly what I need for today. Amen.

DECEMBER 20

God, thank You for Your favor that rests over my life.
This favor replaces luck with love and shows up in
rooms of influence before I ever get there. Amen.

DECEMBER 21

God, thank You for always keeping Your promises and steadying my soul in every season. Please anchor my heart in the hope of Christ. This Christmas, may I never forget Jesus, the One foretold, the One who came, and the One who will come again. Amen.

DECEMBER 22

God, I'm ready to receive Your peace in a deeper and more settling way. Please quiet every anxious thought and make room within me for the Prince of Peace to reign. Help me to walk in communion with You, with others, and within myself. Amen.

DECEMBER 23

God, thank You for the joy that does not depend on circumstances but on Your unchanging presence. Please restore joy to my weary and overwhelmed heart by opening my eyes to recognize the nearness of Christ. Your joy is my strength; may it rise in me, even in unexpected places. Amen.

DECEMBER 24

God, thank You for the gift of Jesus, the perfect expression of Your love made flesh. As I gather with family and friends to celebrate Christmas, please remind me to slow down long enough to adore You with sincerity and gratitude. Keep building in me the desire to reflect Your love in the way I speak, give, and serve. Amen.

DECEMBER 25

Jesus, You are the true reason for the season. You are the Lamb of God. I honor You as we celebrate Your birth. This day marked the change in our lives forever and opened the way for us to be reunited with God. Though You were born into the humblest circumstances, there was nothing ordinary about Your redeeming power. Jesus, today I join Your children across the globe in celebrating Your gift to the world, Your obedience, and the example You set for us. May we return to You with honor, praise, and thanksgiving. Happy birthday, Jesus.

DECEMBER 26

God, yesterday reminded me that Your presence is the true present. Father, forgive me for striving to store up treasures here on earth, forgetting that the real treasure is in heaven. Today, I reset my heart and mind on things above. Teach me to long for the contentment that comes from slowing down and sitting in solitude with You. Amen.

DECEMBER 27

God, thank You for calling me into a deeper relationship with You. I want my life to reflect the truth that communication with You is both an invitation and a response. I will show up with a heart that is open, honest, and willing, trusting that You meet me in every quiet moment and every surrendered word. I'm ready for the restored confidence and steadied spirit that are unlocked only through intimacy with You. Amen.

DECEMBER 28

God, thank You for purifying my passions and breathing fresh purpose into what I do. Thank You for the assignment You've woven into my gifts, my story, and my desire to empower others. I want to walk fully in the calling You have on my life. I am committed to living out what You've placed inside of me with faith, expectation, and obedience. Amen.

DECEMBER 29

God, I want my prayer life to become a living conversation with You. I want it to move my heart, shape my purpose, and draw me closer every day. I will keep making space for You, Lord, by persistently, honestly, and expectantly calling on You. Amen.

DECEMBER 30

God, thank You for inviting me to ask boldly, seek intentionally, and knock faithfully. I take hold of this posture, believing that You hear me and respond in ways that align with Your perfect will. I will keep showing up in prayer with persistence, faith, and expectation, trusting that You honor those who pursue You with a steady and surrendered heart.

Amen.

DECEMBER 31

God, I come before You with a heart of gratitude as I reflect on and fully embrace the highs and the lows of this year. I thank You for the blessings, the lessons, the testing, and the stretching. While there are moments and feelings I still struggle to understand, I trust that Your glory will be revealed in due time. Lord, I ask that You help me carry the culmination of this year into the next. May the joyful moments fill my spirit when I need encouragement, and may the hard lessons remind me to walk in obedience to You and not repeat choices made outside of Your will. God, thank You for it all. Not everyone was granted the blessing to see this last day of the year. For that, I am humbled and grateful. Amen.

MY PRAYER NOTES

MY PRAYER NOTES

MY PRAYER NOTES